Hard Questions About:

By: Only A. Guy

Hard Questions About: God

Published by Only A. Guy Publishing

Cover Art and Editing By Whyte Lady Designs L.L.C.

www.onlyaguy.com
www.facebook.com/onlyaguy
www.twitter.com/onlyaguy1

ISBN 13: 978-0-9847382-0-5
ISBN: 0-9847382-0-5

Printed in the USA.

If you like this book here are some others coming out by this author you may find enjoyable as well as educational:

2011
HARD QUESTIONS ABOUT JESUS
THE BOOK OF PRAYERS
READ THE BIBLE IN A YEAR

2012
HARD QUESTIONS ABOUT THE HOLY SPIRIT
HARD QUESTIONS ABOUT SALVATION
HARD QUESTIONS ABOUT HEAVEN AND HELL
HARD QUESTIONS ABOUT ANGELS AND DEMONS

2013
HARD QUESTIONS ABOUT THE END TIMES
HARD QUESTIONS ABOUT CHRISTIANITY
HARD QUESTIONS ABOUT CREATION
HARD QUESTIONS ABOUT HUMANITY

2014
HARD QUESTIONS ABOUT LIFE'S DESCISIONS
HARD QUESTIONS ABOUT CULTS AND RELIGIONS
HARD QUESTIONS ABOUT FALSE DOCTRINE
HARD QUESTIONS ABOUT PRAYER
HARD QUESTIONS ABOUT SIN

1. Question: "Does God exist? Is there evidence for the existence of God?"

Does God exist? I find it interesting that so much attention is given to this debate. The latest surveys tell us that over 90% of people in the world today believe in the existence of God or some higher power. Yet, somehow the responsibility is placed on those who believe God does exist to somehow prove that He really does exist. To me, I think it should be the other way around.

However, the existence of God cannot be proven or disproved. The Bible even says that we must accept by faith the fact that God exists, *"And without faith it is impossible to please God, because anyone who comes to Him must believe that He exists and that He rewards those who earnestly seek Him" (Hebrews 11:6).* If God so desired, He could simply appear and prove to the whole world that He exists. But if He did that, there would be no need for faith. *"Then Jesus told him, 'Because you have seen me, you have believed; blessed are those who have not seen and yet have believed'" (John 20:29).*

That does not mean, however, that there is a lack of evidence of God's existence. The Bible declares, *"The heavens declare the glory of God; the skies proclaim the work of His hands. Day after day they pour forth speech; night after night they display knowledge. There is no speech or language where their voice is not heard. Their voice goes out into all the earth, their words to the ends of the world" (Psalm 19:1-4).* Looking at the stars, understanding the vastness of the universe, observing the wonders of nature, seeing the beauty of a sunset – all of these things point to a Creator God. If these were not enough, there is also evidence of God in our own hearts. *Ecclesiastes 3:11 tells us, "...He has also set eternity in the hearts of men..."* There is something deep down in our being that recognizes that there is something beyond this life and someone beyond this world. We can deny this knowledge intellectually, but God's presence in us and through us is still there. Despite all of this, the Bible warns us that some will still deny God's existence, *"The fool says in his heart, 'There is no God.'" (Psalm 14:1).* Since over 98% of people throughout history, in all cultures, in all civilizations, on all continents believe in the existence of some kind of God – there must be something (or someone) causing this belief.

In addition to the Biblical arguments for God's existence, there are logical arguments. First, there is the ontological argument. The most popular form of the ontological argument basically uses the concept of God to prove God's existence. It begins with the definition of God as "that than which no greater can be conceived." It is then argued that to exist is greater than to not exist, and therefore the greatest conceivable being must exist. If God did not exist then God would not be the greatest conceivable being - but that would contradict God's very definition.

A second is the teleological argument. The teleological argument is that since the universe displays such an amazing design, there must have been a Divine designer. For example, if earth were even a few hundred miles closer or further away from the sun, it would not be capable of supporting much of the life it currently does. If the elements in our atmosphere were even a few percentage points different, every living thing on earth would die. The odds of a single protein molecule forming by chance is 1 in 10-243 (that is a 10 followed by 243 0's). A single cell is comprised of millions of protein molecules.

A third logical argument for God's existence is called the cosmological argument. Every effect must have a cause. This universe and everything in it is an effect. There must be something that caused everything to come into existence. Ultimately, there must be something "uncaused" in order to cause everything else to come into existence. That "un-caused" something is God.

A fourth argument is known as the moral argument. Every culture throughout history has had some form of law. Everyone has a sense of right and wrong. Murder, lying, stealing, and immorality are almost universally rejected. Where did this sense of right and wrong come from if not from a holy God?

Despite all of this, the Bible tells us that people will reject the clear and undeniable knowledge of God and instead believe a lie. *Romans 1:25 declares, "They exchanged the truth of God for a lie, and worshiped and served created things rather than the Creator - who is forever praised. Amen."* The Bible also proclaims that people are without excuse for not believing in God, *"For since the creation of the world God's invisible qualities - His eternal power and divine nature - have been clearly seen, being understood from what has been made, so that men are without excuse" (Romans 1:20).*

People claim to not believe in God because it is "not scientific" or "because there is no proof." The true reason is that once people admit that there is a God, they also must realize that they are responsible to God and in need of forgiveness from God *(Romans 3:23; 6:23)*. If God exists, then we are accountable for our actions to Him. If God does not exist, then we can do whatever we want without having to worry about God judging us. I believe that is why evolution is so strongly clung to by many in our society - to give people an alternative to believing in a Creator God. God exists and ultimately everyone knows that He exists. The very fact that some attempt so aggressively to disprove His existence is in fact an argument for His existence.

Allow me one last argument for God's existence. How do I know God exists? I know God exists because I speak to Him every day. I do not audibly hear Him speaking back to me, but I sense His presence, I feel His leading, I know His love, I desire His grace. Things have occurred in my life that give no other possible explanation than God. God has so miraculously saved me and changed my life that I cannot help but to acknowledge and praise His existence. None of these arguments in and of themselves can persuade anyone who refuses to acknowledge what is so plainly clear. In the end, God's existence must be accepted by faith *(Hebrews 11:6)*. Faith in God is not a blind leap into the dark; it is safe step into a well-lit room where 90% of people are already standing.

2. Question: "Who is God?"

A. Who is God? - The Fact
The fact of God's existence is so conspicuous, through creation and through man's conscience, that the Bible calls the atheist a "fool" *(Psalm 14:1)*. Accordingly, the Bible never attempts to prove the existence of God; rather, it assumes His existence from the very beginning *(Genesis 1:1)*. What the Bible does is reveal the nature, character, and work of God.

B. Who is God? - The Definition
Thinking correctly about God is of upmost importance because a false idea about God is tantamount to idolatry. In *Psalm 50*, God reproves the wicked man with this accusation: *"you thought I was*

altogether like you" (verse 21). To start with, a good, summary definition of God is "the Supreme Being; the Creator and Ruler of all that is; the Self-existent One who is perfect in power, goodness, and wisdom."

C. Who is God? - His Nature

We know certain things to be true of God for one reason: in His mercy He has condescended to reveal some of His qualities to us. God is spirit, by nature intangible *(John 4:24)*. God is One, but He exists as Three Persons—God the Father, God the Son, and God the Holy Spirit *(Matthew 3:16-17)*. God is infinite *(1 Timothy 1:17)*, incomparable *(2 Samuel 7:22)*, and unchanging *(Malachi 3:6)*. God exists everywhere *(Psalm 139:7-12)*, knows everything *(Matthew 11:21)*, and has all power and authority *(Ephesians 1; Revelation 19:6)*.

D. Who is God? - His Character

Here is some of what the Bible reveals: God is just *(Acts 17:31)*, loving *(Ephesians 2:4-5)*, truthful *(John 14:6)*, and holy *(1 John 1:5)*. God shows compassion *(2 Corinthians 1:3)*, mercy *(Romans 9:15)*, and grace *(Romans 5:17)*. God judges sin *(Psalm 5:5)* but also offers forgiveness *(Psalm 130:4)*.

E. Who is God? - His Work

We cannot understand God apart from His works, because what God does flows from who He is. Here is an abbreviated list of God's works, past, present, and future: God created the world *(Isaiah 42:5)*, He actively sustains the world *(Colossians 1:17)*, He is executing His eternal plan *(Ephesians 1:11)* which involves the redemption of man from the curse of sin and death *(Galatians 3:13-14)*, He draws people to Christ *(John 6:44)*, He disciplines His children *(Hebrews 12:6)*, and He will judge the world *(Revelation 20:11-15)*.

F. Who is God? - A Relationship with Him

In the Person of the Son, God became incarnate *(John 1:14)*. The Son of God became the Son of Man and is therefore the "bridge" between God and man *(John 14:6; 1 Timothy 2:5)*. It is only through the Son that we can have forgiveness of sins *(Ephesians 1:7)*, reconciliation with God *(John 15:15; Romans 5:10)*, and eternal salvation *(2 Timothy 2:10)*. In Jesus Christ *"all the fullness of the Deity lives in bodily form" (Colossians 2:9).* So, to really know who God is, all we have to do is look at Jesus.

3. Question: "Is God real? How can I know for sure that God is real?"

We know that God is real because He has revealed Himself to us in three ways: in creation, in His Word, and in His Son, Jesus Christ.

The most basic proof of God's existence is simply what He has made. *"For the invisible things of Him from the creation of the world are clearly seen, being understood by the things that are made, even His eternal power and Godhead; so that [unbelievers] are without excuse" (Romans 1:20). "The heavens declare the glory of God/And the firmament sheweth His handiwork" (Psalm 19:1)*

If I found a wristwatch in the middle of a field, I would not assume that it just "appeared" out of nowhere or that it had always existed. Based on the watch's design, I would assume it had a designer. But I see far greater design and precision in the world around us. Our measurement of time is not based on wristwatches, but on God's handiwork—the regular rotation of the earth (and the radioactive properties of the cesium-133 atom). The universe displays great design, and this argues for a Great Designer.

If I found an encoded message, I would seek out a cryptographer to help break the code. My assumption would be that there is an intelligent sender of the message, someone who created the code. How complex is the DNA "code" that we carry in every cell of our bodies? Does not the complexity and purpose of DNA argue for an Intelligent Writer of the code?

Not only has God made an intricate and finely tuned physical world, He has also instilled a sense of eternity in the heart of every person *(Ecclesiastes 3:11).* Mankind has an innate perception that there is more to life than meets the eye, that there is an existence higher than this earthly routine. Our sense of eternity manifests itself in at least two ways: law-making and worship.

Every civilization throughout history has valued certain moral laws, which are surprisingly similar from culture to culture. For example, the ideal of love is universally esteemed, while the act of lying is universally condemned. This common morality—this global understanding of right and wrong—points to a Supreme Moral Being who gave us such scruples.

In the same way, people all over the world, regardless of culture, have always cultivated a system of worship. The object of worship may vary, but the sense of a "higher power" is an undeniable part of being human. Our propensity to worship accords with the fact that God created us "in His own image" *(Genesis 1:27)*.

God has also revealed Himself to us through His Word, the Bible. Throughout scripture, the existence of God is treated as a self-evident fact *(Genesis 1:1; Exodus 3:14)*. When Benjamin Franklin wrote his Autobiography, he did not waste time trying to prove his own existence. Likewise, God does not spend much time proving His existence in His book. The life-changing nature of the Bible, its integrity, and the miracles which accompanied its writing should be enough to warrant a closer look.

The third way in which God revealed Himself is through His Son, Jesus Christ *(John 14:6-11)*. *"In the beginning was the Word: the Word was with God, and the Word was God... And the Word was made flesh, and dwelt among us" (John 1:1, 14)*. In Jesus Christ *"dwelleth all the fullness of the Godhead bodily" (Colossians 2:9)*.

In Jesus' amazing life, He kept the entire Old Testament law perfectly and fulfilled the prophecies concerning the Messiah *(Matthew 5:17)*. He performed countless acts of compassion and public miracles to authenticate His message and bear witness to His deity *(John 21:24-25)*. Then, three days after His crucifixion, He rose from the dead, a fact affirmed by hundreds of eyewitnesses *(1 Corinthians 15:6)*. The historical record abounds with "proof" of who Jesus is. As the Apostle Paul said, *"This thing was not done in a corner" (Acts 26:26)*.

We realize that there will always be skeptics who have their own ideas concerning God and will read the evidence accordingly. And there will be some whom no amount of proof will convince *(Psalm 14:1)*. It all comes down to faith *(Hebrews 11:6)*.

4. Question: "Is God dead?"

The technical term for the teaching that "God is dead" is theothanatology, a three-fold compound from the Greek: Theos (god) + Thanatos (death) + logia (word).

German poet and philosopher Friedrich Nietzsche is most famous for making the statement "God is dead" in the Nineteenth Century. Nietzsche, influenced by both Greek philosophy and the theory of evolution, wrote, "God is dead. God remains dead. And we have killed him. How shall we, murderers of all murderers, console ourselves? Is not the greatness of this deed too great for us? Must we not ourselves become gods simply to be worthy of it?" *(Nietzsche, "The Gay Science", §125).*

Nietzsche's purpose was to abolish "traditional" morality, Christianity in particular. In his mind, it represented an attempt of self-serving religious leaders to control the weak and unthinking masses. Nietzsche believed that the "idea" of God was no longer necessary; in fact, God was irrelevant because man was evolving to a place where he could create a deeper and more satisfying "master morality" of his own.

Nietzsche's "God is dead" philosophy has been used to advance the theories of existentialism, nihilism, and socialism. Radical theologians such as Thomas J. J. Altizer and Paul van Buren advocated the "God is dead" idea in the 1960s and 1970s.

The belief that God is dead and religion is irrelevant naturally leads to the following ideas:

A. If God is dead, there are no moral absolutes and no universal standard to which all men should conform.
B. If God is dead, there is no purpose or rational order in life.

C. If God is dead, any design seen in the universe is projected by men who are desperate to find meaning in life.
D. If God is dead, man is independent and totally free to create his own values.
E. If God is dead, the "real" world (as opposed to a heaven and hell) is man's only concern.

The idea that "God is dead" is primarily a challenge to God's authority over our lives. The notion that we can safely create our own rules was the lie that the serpent told Eve: *"ye shall be as gods" (Genesis 3:5).* Peter warns us that *"there shall be false teachers among you, who privily shall bring in damnable heresies, even denying the Lord that bought them, and bring upon themselves swift destruction" (2 Peter 2:1).*

The "God is dead" argument is usually presented as a rational, empowering philosophy for artists and intellectuals. But scripture calls it foolish. *"The fool hath said in his heart, 'There is no God'" (Psalm 14:1).* Ironically, those who hold to the "God is dead" philosophy will discover the fatal error in the philosophy when they themselves are dead.

5. Question: "What are the attributes of God? What is God like?"

The good news, as we try to answer this question, is that there is much that can be found out about God! Those who examine this explanation may find it helpful to first read through it entirely; then go back and look up selected Scripture passages for further clarification. The Scripture references are completely necessary, for without the authority of the Bible, this collection of words would be no better than man's opinion; which by itself is often incorrect in understanding God *(Job 42:7).* To say that it is important for us to try to understand what God is like is a huge understatement! Failure to do so will likely cause us to set up, chase after, and worship false gods contrary to His will *(Exodus 20:3-5).*

Only what God has chosen of Himself to be revealed can be known. One of God's attributes or qualities is "light", meaning that He is self-revealing in information of Himself *(Isaiah 60:19, James 1:17)*. The reality that God has revealed knowledge of Himself should not be neglected, lest anyone of us come short of entering His rest *(Hebrews 4:1)*. Creation, the Bible, and the Word made flesh (Jesus Christ) will help us to know what God is like.

Let's start by understanding that God is our Creator and that we are a part of His creation *(Genesis 1:1 Psalm 24:1)*. God said that man is created in His image. Man is above the rest of creation and was given dominion over it *(Genesis 1:26-28)*. Creation is marred by the 'fall' but still offers a glimpse of His works *(Genesis 3:17-18; Romans 1:19-20)*. By considering creation's vastness, complexity, beauty, and order we can have a sense of the awesomeness of God.

Reading through some of the names of God can be helpful in our search of what God is like. They are as follows:

⇒ Elohim - strong One, divine *(Genesis 1:1)*
⇒ Adonai - Lord, indicating a Master to servant relationship *(Exodus 4:10,13)*
⇒ El Elyon - Most High, the strongest One *(Genesis 14:20)*
⇒ El Roi - the strong One who sees *(Genesis 16:13)*
⇒ El Shaddai - Almighty God *(Genesis 17:1)*
⇒ El Olam - everlasting God *(Isaiah 40:28)*
⇒ Yahweh - LORD "I Am", meaning the eternal self-existent God *(Exodus 3:13,14)*.

We will now continue by examining more of God's attributes; God is eternal, meaning He had no beginning and that His existence will never end. He is immortal, infinite *(Deuteronomy 33:27; Psalm 90:2; 1 Timothy 1:17)*. God is immutable, meaning He is unchangeable; this means that God is absolutely reliable and trustworthy *(Malachi 3:6; Numbers 23:19; Psalm 102:26 & 27)*. God is incomparable, meaning there is no one like Him in works or being; He is unequaled and perfect *(2 Samuel 7:22; Psalm 86:8; Isaiah 40:25; Matthew 5:48)*. God is inscrutable, meaning He is unfathomable, unsearchable, past finding out in entirely understanding Him *(Isaiah 40:28; Psalm 145:3; Romans 11:33 & 34)*.

God is just, meaning He is no respecter of persons in the sense of showing favoritism *(Deuteronomy 32:4; Psalm 18:30)*. God is omnipotent, meaning He is all-powerful; He can do anything that pleases Him, but His actions will always be in accord with the rest of His character *(Revelation 19:6; Jeremiah 32:17 & 27)*. God is omnipresent, meaning He is ever-present, everywhere; this does not mean that God is everything *(Psalm 139:7-13; Jeremiah 23:23)*. God is omniscient, meaning He knows the past, present, and future, even what we are thinking at any given moment; since He knows everything His justice will always be administered fairly *(Psalm 139:1-5; Proverbs 5:21)*.

God is one, meaning not only that there is no other, but also that He is alone in being able to meet the deepest needs and longings of our hearts, and He alone is worthy of our worship and devotion *(Deuteronomy 6:4)*. God is righteous, meaning that God cannot and will not pass over wrongdoing; it is because of His righteousness and justice that in order for our sins to be forgiven, Jesus had to experience God's judgment when our sins were placed upon Him *(Exodus 9:27; Matthew 27:45-46; Romans 3:21-26)*.

God is sovereign, meaning He is supreme; all of His creation put together, whether knowingly or unknowingly, cannot thwart His purposes *(Psalm 93:1; 95:3; Jeremiah 23:20)*. God is spirit, meaning He is invisible *(John 1:18; 4:24)*. God is a Trinity, meaning He is three in one, same in substance, equal in power and glory. Notice that in the first Scripture passage cited that 'name' is singular even though it refers to three distinct Persons- "Father, Son, Holy Spirit" *(Matthew 28:19; Mark 1:9-11)*. God is truth, meaning that He is in agreement with all that He is, He will remain incorruptible and cannot lie *(Psalm 117:2; 1 Samuel 15:29)*.

God is holy, meaning that He is separated from all moral defilement and is hostile toward it. God sees all evil and it angers Him; fire is usually mentioned in scripture along with holiness. God is referred to as a consuming fire *(Isaiah 6:3; Habakkuk 1:13; Exodus 3:2,4 & 5; Hebrews 12:29)*. God is gracious - this would include His goodness, kindness, mercy, and love - which are words that give shades of meaning to His goodness. If it were not for God's grace it would seem that the rest of His attributes would exclude us from Him. Thankfully this is not the case, for He desires to know each of us personally *(Exodus 34:6; Psalm 31:19; 1 Peter 1:3; John 3:16; John 17:3)*.

This has been only a modest attempt to answer a God-sized question. Please be greatly encouraged to continue seeking after Him *(Jeremiah 29:13)*.

6. Question: "What does the Bible teach about the Trinity?"

The most difficult thing about the Christian concept of the Trinity is that there is no way to adequately explain it. The Trinity is a concept that is impossible for any human being to fully understand, let alone explain. God is infinitely greater than we are, therefore we should not expect to be able to fully understand Him. The Bible teaches that the Father is God, that Jesus is God, and that the Holy Spirit is God. The Bible also teaches that there is only one God. Though we can understand some facts about the relationship of the different persons of the Trinity to one another, ultimately, it is incomprehensible to the human mind. However, this does not mean it is not true or not based on the teachings of the Bible.

Keep in mind when studying this subject that the word "Trinity" is not used in Scripture. This is a term that is used to attempt to describe the triune God, the fact that there are 3 coexistent, co-eternal persons that make up God. Understand that this is NOT in any way suggesting 3 Gods. The Trinity is 1 God made up of 3 persons. There is nothing wrong with using the term "Trinity" even though the word is not found in the Bible. It is shorter to say the word "Trinity" than to say "3 coexistent, co-eternal persons making up 1 God." If this presents a problem to you, consider this: the word grandfather is not used in the Bible either. Yet, we know there were grandfathers in the Bible. Abraham was the grandfather of Jacob. So don't get hung up on the term "Trinity" itself. What should be of real importance is that the concept that is REPRESENTED by the word "Trinity" does exist in Scripture. With the introduction out of the way, Bible verses will be given in discussion of the Trinity.

A. There is one God: *Deuteronomy 6:4; 1 Corinthians 8:4; Galatians 3:20; 1 Timothy 2:5.*

B. The Trinity consists of three Persons: *Genesis 1:1; 1:26;*

3:22; 11:7; Isaiah 6:8; 48:16; 61:1; Matthew 3:16-17; Matt 28:19; 2 Corinthians 13:14. In the passages of the Old Testament knowledge of the Hebrew language is helpful. In *Genesis 1:1*, the plural noun "Elohim" is used. In *Genesis 1:26; 3:22; 11:7 and Isaiah 6:8*, the plural pronoun for "us" is used. That "Elohim" and "us" refer to more than two is WITHOUT question. In English, you only have two forms, singular and plural. In Hebrew, you have three forms: singular, dual, and plural. Dual is for two ONLY. In Hebrew, the dual form is used for things that come in pairs like eyes, ears, and hands. The word "Elohim" and the pronoun "us" are plural forms - definitely more than two and therefore must be referring to three or more (Father, Son, Holy Spirit). In *Isaiah 48:16 and 61:1*, the Son is speaking while making reference to the Father and the Holy Spirit. Compare *Isaiah 61:1 to Luke 4:14-19* to see that it is the Son speaking. *Matthew 3:16-17* describes the event of Jesus' baptism. Seen in this is God the Holy Spirit descending on God the Son while God the Father proclaims His pleasure in the Son. *Matthew 28:19 and 2 Corinthians 13:14* are examples of 3 distinct persons in the Trinity.

C. The members of the Trinity are distinguished one from another in various passages: In the Old Testament, "LORD" is distinguished from "Lord" *(Genesis 19:24; Hosea 1:4)*. The "LORD" has a "Son" *(Psalm 2:7, 12; Proverbs 30:2-4)*. Spirit is distinguished from the "LORD" *(Numbers 27:18)* and from "God" *(Psalm 51:10-12)*. God the Son is distinguished from God the Father *(Psalm 45:6-7; Hebrews 1:8-9)*. In the New Testament, *John 14:16-17* is where Jesus speaks to the Father about sending a Helper, the Holy Spirit. This shows that Jesus did not consider Himself to be the Father or the Holy Spirit. Consider also all of the other times in the Gospels where Jesus speaks to the Father. Was He speaking to Himself? No. He spoke to another person in the Trinity - the Father.

D. Each member of the Trinity is God: The Father is God: *John 6:27; Romans 1:7; 1 Peter 1:2.* The Son is God: *John 1:1, 14; Romans 9:5; Colossians 2:9; Hebrews 1:8; 1 John 5:20.* The Holy Spirit is God: *Acts 5:3-4; 1 Corinthians 3:16* (The One who indwells is the Holy Spirit - *Romans 8:9; John 14:16-17; Acts 2:1-4).*

E. The subordination within the Trinity: Scripture shows that the Holy Spirit is subordinate to the Father and the Son, and the Son is subordinate to the Father. This is an internal relationship, and does not deny the deity of any person of the Trinity. This is simply an area which our finite minds cannot understand concerning the infinite God. Concerning the Son see: *Luke 22:42; John 5:36; John 20:21; 1 John 4:14.* Concerning the Holy Spirit see: *John 14:16; 14:26; 15:26; 16:7* and especially *John 16:13-14.*

F. The tasks of the individual members of the Trinity:

The Father is the ultimate source or cause of:
   a. The universe *(1 Corinthians 8:6; Revelation 4:11)*;
   b. Divine revelation *(Revelation 1:1)*;
   c. Salvation *(John 3:16-17)*; and
   d. Jesus' human works *(John 5:17; 14:10).*
The Father INITIATES all of these things.

The Son is the agent through whom the Father does the following works:
   a. The creation and maintenance of the universe *(1 Corinthians 8:6; John 1:3; Colossians 1:16-17)*
   b. Divine revelation *(John 1:1; Matthew 11:27; John 16:12-15; Revelation 1:1)*; and
   c. Salvation *(2 Corinthians 5:19; Matthew 1:21; John 4:42).*
The Father does all these things through the Son, who functions as His agent.

The Holy Spirit is the means by whom the Father does the following works:

a.   Creation and maintenance of the universe *(Genesis 1:2; Job 26:13; Psalm 104:30)*;

b.   Divine revelation *(John 16:12-15; Ephesians 3:5; 2 Peter 1:21)*;

c.   Salvation *(John 3:6; Titus 3:5; 1 Peter 1:2)*; and

d.   Jesus' works *(Isaiah 61:1; Acts 10:38)*.

Thus the Father does all these things by the power of the Holy Spirit.

None of the popular illustrations are completely accurate descriptions of the Trinity. The egg (or apple) fails in that the shell, white, and yolk are parts of the egg, not the egg in themselves. The Father, Son and Holy Spirit are not parts of God, each of them is God. The water illustration is somewhat better but still fails to adequately describe the Trinity. Liquid, vapor, and ice are forms of water. The Father, Son, and Holy Spirit are not forms of God, each of them is God. So, while these illustrations may give us a picture of the Trinity, the picture is not entirely accurate. An infinite God cannot be fully described by a finite illustration. Instead of focusing on the Trinity, try to focus on the fact of God's greatness and infinitely higher nature than our own. *"Oh, the depth of the riches of the wisdom and knowledge of God! How unsearchable his judgments, and his paths beyond tracing out! Who has known the mind of the Lord? Or who has been his counselor?" (Romans 11:33-34)*

7. Question: "Can monotheism be proven?"

A. Definition of Monotheism - Monotheism comes from "mono" (single) and "theism" (the belief in God). Specifically, it is the belief in one true God who is the only creator, sustainer, and judge of all creation. Monotheism differs from henotheism, which is the belief in multiple gods with one supreme God over all. It is also opposed to polytheism, which is the belief in the existence of more than one god. There are many arguments for monotheism, including those from special revelation (Scripture), natural revelation (philosophy), as well as historical anthropology. These will only be explained very briefly below, and this should not in any way be considered an exhaustive list.

B. Biblical arguments for Monotheism

a. *Deuteronomy 4:35*, "You were shown these things so that you might know that the LORD is God; besides Him there is no other."

b. *Deuteronomy 6:4*, "Hear, O Israel: The LORD our God, the LORD is one."

c. *Malachi 2:10a*, "Have we not all one Father? Did not one God create us?"

d. *1 Corinthians 8:6*, "yet for us there is but one God, the Father, from whom all things came and for whom we live; and there is but one Lord, Jesus Christ, through whom all things came and through whom we live."

e. *Ephesians 4:6*, "one God and Father of all, who is over all and through all and in all."

f. *1 Timothy 2:5*, "For there is one God and one mediator between God and men, the man Christ Jesus."

g. *James 2:19*, "You believe that there is one God. Good! Even the demons believe that — and shudder."

Obviously, for many people, it wouldn't do to simply say that there is only one God because the Bible says so. This is because without God there is no way to prove that the Bible is His word in the first place! However, one might argue that, since the Bible has the most reliable supernatural evidence confirming what it teaches, monotheism can be affirmed on these grounds. A similar argument would be the beliefs and teaching of Jesus Christ, who proved that He was God (or at the very least approved by God) by His miraculous birth, life, and the miracle of His resurrection. God cannot lie or be deceived; therefore, what Jesus believed and taught was true. Therefore, monotheism, which Jesus believed and taught, is true. This argument may not be very impressive to those unfamiliar with the case for the supernatural confirmations of Scripture and Christ, but this is a good place to start for one who is familiar with its strength.

C. **Historical arguments for Monotheism** - Arguments from popularity are notoriously suspect, but it is interesting just how much monotheism has affected world religions. The popular evolutionary theory of religious development stems from an evolutionary view of reality in general, and the presupposition of evolutionary anthropology which sees "primitive" cultures as representing the earlier stages of religious development. But there are several problems with this evolutionary theory:

   a. The kind of development it describes has never been observed. In fact, there seems to be no upward development toward monotheism within any culture, actually the opposite seems to be the case.

   b. The anthropological method's definition of "primitive" equates to technological development, yet this is hardly a satisfactory criterion as there are so many components to a given culture.

   c. The alleged stages are often missing or skipped.

   d. Finally, most polytheistic cultures show vestiges of monotheism early in their development. What we find is that this monotheistic God was personal, masculine, lived in the sky, has great knowledge and power, created the world, is the author of morality that we are to obey, that we have disobeyed and are thus estranged from, but has provided a way of reconciliation. Virtually every religion carries a variation of this God at some point in its past before devolving into the chaos of polytheism.

Thus, it seems that most religions began in monotheism and "devolved" into polytheism, animism, and magic, not vice versa. Islam is a very rare case, having come full circle back into a monotheistic belief. Even with this movement, polytheism is often functionally monotheistic or henotheistic. It is a rare polytheistic religion which does not hold one of its gods as sovereign over the rest, with the lesser gods only functioning as intermediaries.

D. **Philosophical / Theological arguments for Monotheism** There are many philosophical arguments for the impossibility of there being more than one God in existence. Many of these depend a great deal on one's metaphysical position concerning the nature of reality. Unfortunately, in an article this short it would be impossible to argue for these basic metaphysical positions and then go on to show what they point to regarding monotheism, but rest assured that there are strong philosophical and theological grounds for these truths that go back millennia (and most are fairly self-evident). Briefly, then, here are three arguments one might choose to explore (in rough order of difficulty):

   a. If there were more than one God, then the universe would be in disorder because of multiple creators and authorities, but it is not in disorder; therefore, there is only one God.

   b. Since God is a completely perfect being, then there cannot be a second God, for they would have to differ in some way, and to differ from complete perfection is to be less than perfect and not be God.

   c. Since God is infinite in His existence, then He cannot have parts (for parts cannot be added to reach infinity). If God's existence is not just a part of Him (which it is for all things which can have existence or not), then He must have infinite existence. Therefore, there cannot be two infinite beings, for one would have to differ from the other, and to differ from infinite existence is to not exist at all.

Someone may wish to argue that many of these would not rule out a sub-class of "gods," and that's fine. Although we know this to be untrue biblically, there is nothing wrong with it in theory. In other words God could have created a sub-class of "gods," but it just happens to be the case that He did not. If He had, these "gods" would only be limited, created things – probably a lot like angels *(cf. Psalm 82)*. This does not hurt the case for monotheism, which does not say that there cannot be any other spirit beings – only that there cannot be another actual God.

8. Question: "What is theology proper/Paterology?"

Theology proper is the study of God and His attributes. Theology proper focuses on God the Father. Paterology comes from two Greek words meaning "father" & "word" which combine to mean "the study of the Father."

Theology proper answers several important questions about God:

A. **Does God exist?** God exists and ultimately everyone knows that He exists. The very fact that some attempt so aggressively to disprove His existence is in fact an argument for His existence.

B. **What are the attributes of God?** In the words of the hymn writer, "immortal, invisible, God only wise.most blessed, most glorious, the Ancient of Days, Almighty, Victorious, thy great name we praise." Knowing God's attributes leads to glorifying and praising Him.

C. **What does the Bible teach about the Trinity?** Though we can understand some facts about the relationship of the different persons of the Trinity to one another, ultimately, it is incomprehensible to the human mind. However, this does not mean it is not true or not based on the teachings of the Bible.

D. **Is God sovereign, or do we have a free will?** When we

talk about free will, we are usually concerned with the matter of salvation. Few are interested in whether we have the free will to choose salad or steak for our dinner tonight. Rather, we are troubled over who exactly is in control of our eternal destiny.

Theology proper discusses God's omnipresence, omniscience, omnipotence, and eternality. It teaches us about who God is and what He does.

Paterology focuses on how God the Father is distinct from God the Son and God the Holy Spirit. Only by knowing who God is and what He does can we properly relate to Him. Many people have unbiblical perceptions about God that affects how they understand Him. Some people see God as a brutal tyrant, with no love or grace. Other people see God as a loving friend, with no justice or anger. Both perceptions are equally incorrect. God is full of mercy, love, and grace - and at the same time righteous, holy, and just. God grants mercy and sends judgment. God punishes sin and forgives sin. God will grant believers entrance into Heaven and send unbelievers to Hell.

Romans 11:33 is perhaps a good summary verse for theology proper/ Paterology: *"Oh, the depth of the riches of the wisdom and knowledge of God! How unsearchable his judgments, and his paths beyond tracing out"*

9. Question: "Why does God allow bad things to happen to good people?"

Why do bad things happen to good people? That is one of the difficult questions in all of theology. God is eternal, infinite, omniscient, omnipresent, omnipotent, etc. Why should we human beings (not eternal, infinite, omniscient, omnipresent, or omnipotent) expect to be able to fully understand God's ways?

The book of Job deals with this issue. God had allowed Satan to do everything he wanted to Job except kill him. What was Job's reaction? *"Though he slay me, yet will I hope in him" (Job 13:15). "The LORD* gave and the LORD has taken away; may the name of the LORD be praised" (Job 1:21). Job didn't understand why God had allowed the things He did, but he knew that God was good and therefore continued to trust in Him. Ultimately, that should be our reaction as well. God is good, just, loving, and merciful. Often things happen to us that we simply cannot understand. However, instead of doubting God's goodness, our reaction should be to trust Him. *"Trust in the LORD with all your heart and lean not on your own understanding; in all your ways acknowledge Him, and He will make your paths straight" (Proverbs 3:5-6).*

Perhaps a better question is, "Why do good things happen to bad people?" God is holy *(Isaiah 6:3; Revelation 4:8)*. Human beings are sinful *(Romans 3:23; 6:23)*. Do you want to know how God views humanity? *"As it is written: There is no one righteous, not even one; there is no one who understands, no one who seeks God. All have turned away, they have together become worthless; there is no one who does good, not even one. Their throats are open graves; their tongues practice deceit. The poison of vipers is on their lips. Their mouths are full of cursing and bitterness. Their feet are swift to shed blood; ruin and misery mark their ways, and the way of peace they do not know. There is no fear of God before their eyes" (Romans 3:10-18)*. Every human being on this planet deserves to be thrown into hell at this very moment. Every second we spend alive is only by the grace of God. Even the most terrible misery we could experience on this planet is merciful compared to what we deserve, eternal hell in the lake of fire.

"But God demonstrates his own love for us in this: While we were still sinners, Christ died for us" (Romans 5:8). Despite the evil, wicked, sinful nature of the people of this world, God still loved us. He loved us enough to die to take the penalty for our sins *(Romans 6:23)*. All we have to do is believe in Jesus Christ *(John 3:16; Romans 10:9)* in order to be forgiven and promised a home in heaven *(Romans 8:1)*. What we deserve = hell. What we are given = eternal life in heaven if we would just believe.

It has been said, this world is the only hell believers will ever experience, and this world is the only heaven unbelievers will ever experience. The next time we ask the question, "Why does God allow bad things to happen to good people?" maybe we should be asking, "Why does God allow good things to happen to bad people?"

10. Question: "Did God create evil?"

At first it might seem that if God created all things then evil must have been created by God. However, there is an assumption here that needs to be cleared up. Evil is not a "thing" like a rock or a river. You can't have a jar of evil! Rather, evil is something that occurs, like running.

Evil has no existence of its own - it is really a lack in a good thing. For example, holes are real but they only exist in something else. We call the absence of dirt a hole - but it cannot be separated from the dirt. So when God created, it is true that, all that existed was good. One of the good things God made were creatures that had the freedom to choose good. In order to have a real choice, God had to allow there to be something besides good to choose. So God allowed these free angels and humans to choose good or non-good (evil). When a bad relationship exists between two good things we call that evil, but it does not become a "thing" that required God to create it.

Perhaps a further illustration will help. If I were to ask the average person "does cold exist?" his/her answer would likely be yes. However, this is incorrect. Cold does not exist. Cold is the absence of heat. Similarly, darkness does not exist. Darkness is the absence of light. Similarly, evil is the absence of good, or better, evil is the absence of God. God did not have to create evil, but rather only allow for the absence of good, or the absence of his presence in our being.

Look at the example of Job in Job chapters 1-2. Satan wanted to destroy Job, and God allowed Satan to do everything but kill Job. God allowed this to happen to prove to Satan that Job was righteous because he loved God, not because God had blessed him so richly. God is sovereign and ultimately in control of everything that happens. Satan cannot do anything that God does not allow. God did not create evil, but He allows evil. If God had not allowed for the possibility of evil, both mankind and angels would be serving God out of obligation, not choice. He did not want "robots" that simply did what He wanted them to do because of their "programming." God allowed for the possibility of evil so that we could genuinely have a free will and choose whether we wanted to serve Him or not.

Ultimately, there is not an answer to these questions that we can fully comprehend. We, as finite human beings, can never fully understand an infinite God *(Romans 11:33-34)*. Sometimes we think we understand why God is doing something, only to find out later that it was for a different purpose than we originally thought. God looks at things from an eternal perspective. We look at things from an earthly perspective. Why did God put man on earth knowing that Adam and Eve would sin and therefore bring evil, death, and suffering on all mankind? Why didn't He just create us all and leave us in Heaven where we would be perfect and without suffering? The best answer I can come up with is this: God didn't want a race of robots that did not have a free will. God had to allow the possibility of evil for us to have a true choice of whether to worship God or not. If we never had to suffer and experience evil, would we truly know how wonderful heaven is? God did not create evil, but He allowed it. If He hadn't allowed evil, we would be worshipping Him out of obligation, not by a choice of our own free will.

11. Question: "Why does God allow the innocent to suffer?"

In answering this question, the first thing to consider is whether such a thing as "the innocent" even exists. According to the Bible, *"the heart is wicked and deceitful above all things" (Jeremiah 17:9)*, and *"all have sinned and fallen short of the glory of God" (Romans 3:23)*. Therefore, no one is innocent in the sense of being sinless. Sin entered the world when Adam and Even rebelled against God in the Garden of Eden, and mankind has been in rebellion ever since. Sin's effects permeate everything, and the suffering we see all around us is a direct result of that sin.

But God did not leave us here to suffer pointlessly. Our loving and merciful God has a perfect plan to use that suffering to accomplish His threefold purpose. First, He uses pain and suffering to draw us to Himself so that we will cling to Him. Jesus said, *"In the world you shall have tribulation" (John 16:33)*. Trials and distress are not something unusual in life; they are part of what it means to be human in a fallen world. In Christ we have an anchor that holds fast in all the storms of life, but if we never sail into those storms, how would we know that? It is in times of despair and sorrow that we reach out to Him, and, if we are His children, we always find Him there waiting to comfort and uphold us through it all. In this way, He proves His faithfulness to us and ensures that we will stay close to Him. An added benefit is that as we experience God's comfort through trials, we are then able to comfort others in the same way *(2 Corinthians 1:4)*.

Second, He proves to us that our faith is real through the suffering and pain that are inevitable in this life. How we respond to suffering is determined by the genuineness of our faith. Those with faith truly from God, *"the author and finisher of our faith" (Hebrews 12:2)*, will not be crushed by suffering, but will come through the trial with their faith intact, having been *"proven through fire"* so that it *"might be found to praise and honor and glory at the revelation of Jesus Christ" (1 Peter 1:7)*. Those are the ones who do not shake their fists at God or question His goodness, but instead *"count it all joy" (James 1:2)*, knowing that trials prove that they are truly the children of God. *"Blessed is the man who endures temptation, because having been approved, he will receive the crown of life which the Lord has promised to those who love Him" (James 1:12)*.

Finally, God uses suffering to take our eyes off this world and put them on the next. The Bible continually exhorts us to not get caught up in the things of this world, but to look forward to the world to come. This world and all that is in it will pass away, but the kingdom of God is eternal. Jesus said, *"My kingdom is not of this world" (John 18:36)*, and those who would follow Him must not see the things of this life, both good and bad, as the end of the story. Even the sufferings we endure and which seem so terrible *"are not worthy to be compared with the coming glory to be revealed in us" (Romans 8:18)*.

Could God prevent all suffering? Of course He could! But, He assures us that *"all things work together for good to those who love God and are called according to His purpose" (Romans 8:28)*. So even suffering is part of the "all things" that God is using to accomplish His good purposes. His plan is perfect, His character is flawless, and those who trust Him will not be disappointed.

12. Question: "Does God love everyone or just Christians?"

There is a sense in which God loves everyone in the whole world *(John 3:16; 1 John 2:2; Romans 5:8)*. This love is not conditional, it is based only on the fact that God is a God of love *(1 John 4:8 & 16)*. God's love for all of mankind results in the fact that God shows His mercy by not immediately punishing people for their sins *(Romans 3:23; 6:23)*. If God did not love everyone, we would all be in hell right now. God's love for the world is manifested in the fact that He gives people the opportunity to repent *(2 Peter 3:9)*. However, God's love for the world does not mean that He will ignore sin. God is also a God of justice *(2 Thessalonians 1:6)*. Sin cannot go unpunished forever *(Romans 3:25-26)*.

The most loving act of eternity is described in *Romans 5:8*, "But God demonstrates His own love for us in this: While we were still sinners, Christ died for us." Anyone who ignores God's love, who rejects Christ as Savior, who denies the Savior who bought him *(2 Peter 2:1)* that person will be subject to God's wrath for eternity *(Romans 1:18)*, not His love *(Romans 6:23)*. God loves everyone unconditionally in that He shows mercy to everyone. God conditionally loves only those who place their faith in His Son for salvation *(John 3:36)*. Only those who believe in Jesus Christ as their Lord and Savior will experience God's love for eternity.

Does God love everyone? Yes. Does God love Christians more than He loves non-Christians? No. Does God love Christians differently than He loves non-Christians? Yes. God loves everyone equally in that He is merciful to all. God only loves Christians in that Christians have His eternal grace and mercy, the promise of His forever love in Heaven. It is God's love for all that should draw us all to receive His eternal love.

13. Question: "Is God sovereign or do we have a free will?"

When we talk about free will, we are usually concerned with the matter of salvation. Few are interested in whether we have the free will to choose salad or steak for our dinner tonight. Rather, we are troubled over who exactly is in control of our eternal destiny.

Any discussion of man's free will must begin with an understanding of his nature because man's will is bound by that nature. A prisoner has the freedom to pace up and down in his cell, but he is constrained by the walls of that cell and can go no further, no matter how much his will might desire it. So it is with man. Because of sin, man is imprisoned within a cell of corruption and wickedness which permeates to the very core of our being. Every part of man is in bondage to sin – our bodies, our minds, and our wills. *Jeremiah 17:9* tells us the state of man's heart: it is "deceitful and desperately wicked." In our natural, unregenerate state, we are carnally minded, not spiritually minded. *"For to be carnally minded is death, but to be spiritually minded is life and peace because the carnal mind is enmity against God, for it is not subject to the Law of God, neither indeed can it be" (Romans 8:6-7).* These verses tell us that before we are saved, we are at enmity (war) with God, we do not submit to God and His law, neither can we. The Bible is clear that, in his natural state, man is incapable of choosing that which is good and holy. In other words, he does not have the "free will" to choose God because his will is not free. It is constrained by his nature, just as the prisoner is constrained by his cell.

How then can anyone be saved? *Ephesians 2:1* describes the process. We who are "dead in our trespasses and sins" have been "made alive" through Christ. A dead man cannot make himself alive because he lacks the necessary power to do so. Lazarus lay in his tomb four days unable to do a thing to resurrect himself. Christ came along and commanded him to come to life *(John 11)*. So it is with us. We are spiritually dead, unable to rise. But "while we were yet sinners Christ died for us" *(Romans 5:8)*. He calls us out of our spiritual graves and gives us a completely new nature, one undefiled by sin as the old nature was *(2 Corinthians 5:17)*. God saw the desperate and helpless state of our souls, and in His great love and mercy, He chose, in his sovereignty, to send His Son to the cross to redeem us. By His grace we are saved through the gift of faith which He gives us so that we can believe in Jesus. His grace is a free gift, our faith is a free gift, and our salvation is a free gift given to those whom God has chosen *"before the foundation of the world" (Ephesians 1:4)*. Why did He choose to do it this way? Because, it was *"according to the good pleasure of His will, to the praise of the glory of His grace" (Ephesians 1:5-6)*. It's important to understand that the plan of salvation is designed to glorify God, not man. Our response is to praise Him for the "glory of His grace." If we chose our own salvation, who would get the glory? We would, and God has made it clear that He will not give the glory due to Him to anyone else *(Isaiah 48:11)*.

The question naturally arises, how do we know who has been saved "from the foundation of the world"? We don't. That is why we take the good news of salvation through Jesus Christ to the ends of the earth, telling all to repent and receive God's gift of grace. *2 Corinthians 5:20* tells us we are to be pleading with others to be reconciled to God before it is too late. We cannot know who God will choose to release from their prison cells of sin. We leave that choice to Him and present the Gospel to all. The ones who come to Jesus He *"will in no way cast out" (John 6:37).*

14. Question: "What are the different names of God and what do they mean?"

Each of the many names of God describes a different aspect of His many-faceted character. Here are some of the better known names of God in the Bible:

⇒ **EL, ELOAH**: God *"mighty, strong, prominent" (Genesis 7:1; Isaiah 9:6)* – Etymologically, El appears to mean power, as in *"I have the power to harm you" (Genesis 31:29)*. El is associated with other qualities, such as integrity *(Numbers 23:19)*, jealousy *(Deuteronomy 5:9)*, and compassion *(Nehemiah 9:31)*, but the root idea of might remains.

⇒ **ELOHIM**: God *"Creator, Mighty and Strong" (Genesis 17:7; Jeremiah 31:33)* – The plural form of Eloah, which is accommodating of the doctrine of the Trinity. From the Bible's first sentence, the superlative nature of God's power is evident as God (Elohim) speaks the world into existence *(Genesis 1:1)*.

⇒ **EL SHADDAI**: "God Almighty," "The Mighty One of Jacob" *(Genesis 49:24; Psalm 132:2 & 5)* – Speaks to God's ultimate power over all.

⇒ **ADONAI**: "Lord" *(Genesis 15:2; Judges 6:15)* – Used in place of YHWH, which was thought by the Jews to be too sacred to be uttered by sinful men. In the Old Testament, YHWH is more often used in God's dealings with His people, while Adonai is used more when He deals with the Gentiles.

⇒ **YHWH / YAHWEH / JEHOVAH**: "LORD" *(Deuteronomy 6:4; Daniel 9:14)* – Strictly speaking, the only proper name for God. When translated in English Bibles "LORD" (all capitals) is used to distinguish from Adonai "Lord." The revelation of the name is first given to Moses "I Am who I Am" *(Exodus 3:14)*. This name specifies immediacy, a presence. Yahweh is present, accessible, near to those who call on Him for deliverance *(Psalm 107:13)*, forgiveness *(Psalm 25:11)* and guidance *(Psalm 31:3)*.

⇒ **YAHWEH-JIREH**: "The Lord will Provide" *(Genesis 22:14)* – The name memorialized by Abraham when God provided the ram to be sacrificed in place of Isaac.

⇒ **YAHWEH-RAPHA**: "The Lord Who Heals" *(Exodus 15:26)* – "I am Jehovah who heals you" both in body and soul. In body, by preserving from diseases, and by curing them when afflicted with them and in soul, by pardoning their iniquities.

⇒ **YAHWEH-NISSI**: "The Lord Our Banner" *(Exodus 17:15)*, where banner is understood to be a rallying place. This name commemorates the desert victory over the Amalekites in *Exodus 17*.

⇒ **YAHWEH-M'KADDESH**: "The Lord Who Sanctifies, Makes Holy" *(Leviticus 20:8; Ezekiel 37:28)* – God makes it clear that He alone, not the law, could cleanse His people and make them holy.

⇒ **YAHWEH-SHALOM**: "The Lord Our Peace" *(Judges 6:24)* – The name given by Gideon to the altar he built after the Angel of the Lord assured him he would not die as he thought he would after seeing Him.

⇒ **YAHWEH-ELOHIM**: "LORD God" *(Genesis 2:4; Psalm 59:5)* – Combination of God's unique name YHWH and the generic "Lord," signifying that He is the Lord of Lords.

⇒ **YAHWEH-TSIDKENU**: "The Lord Our Righteousness" *(Jeremiah 33:16)* – As with YHWH-M'Kaddesh, it is God alone who provides righteousness to man, ultimately in the person of His Son, Jesus Christ, who became sin for us *"that we might become the Righteousness of God in Him" (2 Corinthians 5:21)*.

⇒ **YAHWEH-ROHI**: "The Lord Our Shepherd" *(Psalm 23:1)* – After David pondered his relationship as a shepherd to his sheep, he realized that was exactly the relationship God had with him, and so he declares *"Yahweh-Rohi is my Shepherd. I shall not want" (Psalm 23:1)*.

⇒ **YAHWEH-SHAMMAH**: "The Lord is There" i – The name ascribed to Jerusalem and the Temple there, indicating that the once departed glory of the Lord *(Ezekiel 8 - 11)* had returned *(Ezekiel 44:1-4)*.

⇒ **YAHWEH-SABAOTH**: "The Lord of Hosts" *(Isaiah 1:24; Psalm 46:7)* – "Hosts" means hordes, both of angels and of men. He is Lord of the host of heaven, and of the inhabitants of the earth, of Jews and Gentiles, of rich and poor, master and slave. The name is expressive of the majesty, power, and authority of God and shows that he is able to accomplish what he determines to do.

⇒ **EL ELYON**: "Most High" *(Deuteronomy 26:19)* – Derived from the Hebrew root for "go up" or "ascend," so the implication is of that which is the very highest. El Elyon denotes exaltation and speaks of absolute right to lordship

⇒ **EL ROI**: "God of Seeing" *(Genesis 16:13)* – The name ascribed to God by Hagar, alone and desperate in the wilderness after being driven out by Sarah *(Genesis 16:1-14)*, when she met the Angel of the Lord and realized she had seen God Himself in a theophany. She realized that El Roi saw her in her distress and testified that He is a God who lives and sees all.

⇒ **EL-OLAM**: "Everlasting God" *(Psalm 90:1-3)* – God's nature is without beginning or end, free from all constraints of time and contains within Himself the very cause of time itself. "From everlasting to everlasting, You are God."

⇒ **EL-GIBHOR**: "Mighty God" *(Isaiah 9:6)* – The name describing the Messiah, Christ Jesus, in this prophetic portion of Isaiah. As a powerful and mighty warrior, the Messiah, the Mighty God, will accomplish the destruction of God's enemies and rule with a rod of iron *(Revelation 19:15)*.

15. Question: "Where was God on September 11?"

On September 11, 2001, God was exactly where He always is – in Heaven in total control of everything that happens in the universe. Why, then, would a good and loving God allow such a tragedy to happen? This is a more difficult question to answer. First, we must remember, *"For as the heavens are higher than the earth, So are My ways higher than your ways, And My thoughts than your thoughts" (Isaiah 55:9)*. It is impossible for finite human beings to understand the ways of an infinite God *(Romans 11:33-35)*. Second, we must realize that God is not responsible for the wicked acts of evil men. The Bible tells us that humanity is desperately wicked and sinful *(Romans 3:10-18, 23)*. God allows human beings to commit sin for His own reasons and to fulfill His own purposes. Sometimes we think we understand why God is doing something, only to find out later that it was for a different purpose than we originally thought.

God looks at things from an eternal perspective. We look at things from an earthly perspective. Why did God put man on earth, knowing that Adam and Eve would sin and therefore bring evil, death, and suffering on all mankind? Why didn't He just create us all and leave us in Heaven where we would be perfect and without suffering? It must be remembered that the purpose for all creation and all creatures is to glorify God. God is glorified when His nature and attributes are on display. If there were no sin, God would have no opportunity to display His justice and wrath as He punishes sin. Nor would He have the opportunity to show His grace, His mercy, and His love to undeserving creatures. The ultimate display of God's grace was at the Cross where Jesus died for our sins. Here was unselfishness and obedience displayed in His Son who knew no sin but was *"made sin for us that we might become the righteousness of God in Him" (2 Corinthians 5:21)*. This was all to the *"praise of His glory" (Ephesians 1:14)*.

When thinking of September 11, we tend to forget the thousands of miracles that occurred on that day. Hundreds of people were able to flee the buildings just in the nick of time. A small handful of firemen and one civilian survived in a tiny space in a stairwell as the one of the towers collapsed around them. When the passengers on Flight 93 defeated the terrorists that was a miracle in and of itself. Yes, September 11 was a terrible day. Sin reared its ugly head and caused great devastation. However, God is still in control. His sovereignty is never to be doubted. Could God have prevented what happened on September 11?

Of course He could, but He chose to allow the events to unfold exactly as they did. He prevented that day from being as bad as it could have been. Since September 11, how many lives have been changed for the better? How many people have placed their faith in Christ for salvation as a result of what happened? The words of *Romans 8:28* should always be in our minds when we think of 9-11, "And we know that all things work together for good to those who love God, and are called according to His purpose."

16. Question: "Does God still perform miracles?"

When God performed amazing and powerful miracles for the Israelites, did that cause them to obey Him? No, the Israelites constantly disobeyed and rebelled against God even though they saw all the miracles. The same people who saw God part the Red Sea later doubted whether God was able to conquer the inhabitants of the Promised Land. Read the account in *Luke 16:19-31*. In the story, a man in hell asks Abraham to send Lazarus back from the dead to warn his brothers. Abraham informed the man, "If they do not listen to Moses and the Prophets, they will not be convinced even if someone rises from the dead" *(Luke 16:31)*.

Jesus performed countless miracles, yet the vast majority of people did not believe in Him. If God performed miracles today like He did in the past, the same result would occur. People would be amazed and would believe in God for a short time. That faith would be shallow and would disappear the moment something unexpected or frightening occurred. A faith based on miracles is not a mature faith. God performed the greatest miracle of all time in coming to earth in the Man Jesus Christ, to die on the cross for our sins *(Romans 5:8)*, so that we could be saved *(John 3:16)*. God does still perform miracles - many of them simply go unnoticed or are denied. However, we do not need more miracles. What we need is to believe in the miracle of salvation through faith in Jesus Christ.

Another important concept to understand is the fact that the purpose of miracles was to authenticate the performer of the miracles. *Acts 2:22* declares, *"Men of Israel, listen to this: Jesus of Nazareth was a man accredited by God to you by miracles, wonders and signs, which God did among you through him, as you yourselves know."* The same is said of the Apostles, *"The things that mark an apostle — signs, wonders and miracles — were done among you with great perseverance"* (2 Corinthians 12:12). Speaking of the Gospel, *Hebrews 2:4* proclaims, *"God also testified to it by signs, wonders and various miracles, and gifts of the Holy Spirit distributed according to His will."* We now have the truth of Jesus recorded in Scripture. We now have the writings of the Apostles recorded in Scripture. Jesus and His apostles, as recorded in Scripture, are the cornerstone and foundation of our faith *(Ephesians 2:20)*. In this sense, miracles are no longer necessary, as the message of Jesus and His apostles has already been attested to, and accurately recorded in the Scriptures. Yes, God still performs miracles. At the same time, we should not necessarily expect miracles to occur today just as they did as recorded in the Bible.

17. Question: "Does God hear / answer the prayers of a sinner / unbeliever?"

John 9:31 declares, "We know that God does not hear sinners, but those who worship Him and do His will, those He hears." It has also been said that *"the only prayer that God hears from a sinner is the prayer for salvation."* As a result of this Scripture, some believe that God does not hear and/or will never answer the prayers of an unbeliever. In context, though, the Scripture is saying that God does not perform miracles through an unbeliever. The following Scriptures describe God hearing and answering the prayers of an unbeliever. *1 John 5:14 & 15* tells us that God answers prayers based on whether they are asked according to His will. This principle, perhaps, applies to unbelievers. If an unbeliever asks a prayer of God that is according to His will, nothing prevents God from answering such a prayer – according to His will.

In examining the following passages, in most of these cases prayer was involved. In one or two, God responded to the cry of the heart (it is not stated whether that cry was directed toward God). In some of these cases, the prayer seems to be combined with repentance. But in other cases, the prayer was simply for an earthly need or blessing, and God responded either out of compassion or in response to the genuine seeking or faith of the person. Here are some passages dealing with prayer by an unbeliever:

⇒ The people of Ninevah; *Jonah 3:5-10*; that Ninevah might be spared.
⇒ Hagar and Ishmael; *Genesis 21:14-19*; not so much a prayer as a cry of the heart concerning her son who was close to death.
⇒ Ahab; *1 Kings 21:17-29; esp. v. 27-29*; Ahab fasts and mourns over Elijah's prophecy concerning his posterity. God responds by not bringing about the calamity in Ahab's time.
⇒ The woman from the Tyre and Sidon area; *Mark 7:24-30*; that Jesus would deliver her daughter from a demon.
⇒ Cornelius, the Roman centurion; *Acts 10*; the prayer request is not stated *(Acts 10:30)*, but he is shown the way of salvation.

God does make promises that are applicable for all (saved and unsaved alike) such as *Jeremiah 29:13*: "And ye shall seek me, and find me, when ye shall search for me with all your heart." This was the case for Cornelius in *Acts 10:1-6*. But there are many promises that, according to the context of the passages, are for Christians alone. Because Christians have received Christ, we are encouraged to come boldly unto the throne of grace to find help in time of need *(Hebrews 4:14-16)*. We are told that when we ask for anything according to God's will, He hears and gives us what we ask for *(1 John 5:14-15)*. There are many other promises for Christians concerning prayer as well *(Matthew 21:22; John 14:13; John 15:7)*. So, yes, there are instances in which God does not answer the prayers of an unbeliever. At the same time, in His grace and mercy, God can intervene in the lives of unbelievers in response to their prayers.

18. Question: "Why does God love us?"

This short question is among the most profound questions ever asked. And no human would ever be able to answer it sufficiently. One thing is certain, however. God does not love us because we are lovable or because we deserve His love. If anything, the opposite is true. The state of mankind since the fall is one of rebellion and disobedience. *Jeremiah 17:9 describes man's inner condition: "The heart is deceitful and desperately wicked. Who can know it?"* Our innermost beings are so corrupted by sin that even we don't realize the extent to which sin has tainted us. In our natural state, we do not seek God; we do not love God; we do not desire God. *Romans 3:10-12 clearly presents the state of the natural, unregenerate person: "There is none righteous, no, not one; There is none who understands; There is none who seeks after God. They have all turned aside; They have together become unprofitable; There is none who does good, no, not one."* How then is it possible for a holy, righteous, and perfect God to love such creatures? To understand this we must understand something of the nature and character of God.

First *John 4:8 & 16* tell us that "God is love." Never was a more important declaration made than this; never was more meaning crowded into a few words than in this short sentence - God is love. This is a profound statement. God doesn't just love; He is love. His nature and essence are love. Love permeates His very being and infuses all His other attributes, even His wrath and anger. Because God's very nature is love, He must demonstrate love, just as He must demonstrate all His attributes because doing so glorifies Him. Glorifying God is the highest, the best, and the most noble of all acts, so, naturally, glorifying Himself is what He must do, because He is the highest and the best, and He deserves all glory.

Since it is God's essential nature to love, He demonstrates His love by lavishing it on undeserving people who are in rebellion against Him. God's love is not a sappy, sentimental, romantic feeling. Rather, it is agape love, the love of self-sacrifice. He demonstrates this sacrificial love by sending His Son to the cross to pay the penalty for our sin *(1 John 4:10)*, by drawing us to Himself *(John 6:44)*, by forgiving us of our rebellion against Him, and by sending His Holy Spirit to dwell within us, thereby enabling us to love as He loves. He did this in spite of the fact that we did not deserve it. *"But God demonstrates His own love for us in this: While we were still sinners, Christ died for us" (Romans 5:8).*

God's love is personal. He knows each of us individually and loves us personally. His is a mighty love that has no beginning and no end. It is this experiencing of God's love that distinguishes Christianity from all other religions. Why does God love us? It is because of who He is: "God is love."

19. Question: "Why was God so evident in the Bible, and seems so hidden today?"

The Bible records God appearing to people, performing amazing and undeniable miracles, speaking audibly, and many other things that we do not seem to witness today. Why is this? Why was God so willing to reveal and prove Himself in Bible times, but almost seems "hidden" and silent today? God used miracles and direct communication with people in order to reveal to them His character and nature, as well as His plans and commands. His first miracle, creation, was the primary evidence of God's existence and exhibited many of His attributes. From what was made, man could conclude that God is powerful, sovereign, and good. The creation was His first declaration to mankind. *"The heavens declare the glory of God; and the expanse proclaims His handiwork" (Psalm 19:1).* Following creation, God spoke to people to further declare Himself and to inform man of His law and His ways. He first spoke to Adam and Eve, giving them commandments to follow and, when they disobeyed, pronouncing a curse upon them and their descendants. He also assured them, and all mankind, that He would send a Savior to redeem us from sin. Thereafter, God spoke to Moses, giving him the law for His people to follow. He performed miracle after miracle to verify His existence to His people and to build their faith in Him. In addition, He spoke to His prophets so they would write down His words, words which were preserved for us in the Bible.

When Jesus came to earth, He also performed miracles to prove that He was indeed the Son of God and to foster belief in Him *(Matthew 9:6; John 10:38).* After His miraculous resurrection, He enabled His disciples to continue performing miracles in order to prove they were truly His, again so that people would believe on Him who sent them. So why does God no longer speak audibly to us?

There are several reasons for this. As noted above, God has already spoken, and His words have been miraculously kept for us down through the ages. Now we have the completed canon of scripture, and we need no further miracles to "validate" the Bible. In His perfect Word is everything we need *"for doctrine, for reproof, for correction and instruction in righteousness" (2 Timothy 3:16)*. The Bible is complete and is perfectly able to make us *"wise to salvation through faith in Christ Jesus" (2 Timothy 3:15)*, a *"more sure Word of prophecy to which we would do well to take heed" (2 Peter 1:19)*. We need nothing more, and we are not to seek extra-biblical revelations. To do so calls into question the efficacy of Scripture which God has declared to be sufficient.

Second, we have within us the Holy Spirit whom God has given to us to *"lead us into all truth" (John 16:13)*. He speaks to us continually, teaching us *(1 Corinthians 2:3)*, reminding us of all things that Jesus taught *(John 14:26)*, guiding, correcting, and convicting us of sin *(John 16:8)*. God is indeed "speaking" to us today through the Holy Spirit, who is certainly not hidden. Another reason for God's seeming concealment is alluded to by the prophet Habakkuk: *"The just shall live by his faith" (Habakkuk 2:4)*. God does not give His people a continual chain of miraculous signs; He expects them to trust what He has already done, search the Scriptures daily, respond to the Holy Spirit within, and live by faith, not by sight *(Matthew 16:4; John 20:29)*.

Finally, let us remember that even in those times when it seems that God is doing nothing, He is still the sovereign Lord of all creation, and He is constantly at work, bringing about the fruition of His perfect plan. One of the best examples of God's "hidden" working is the book of Esther, in which God is never mentioned, but which plainly shows His sovereign hand at work from beginning to end.

20. Question: "Does God punish us when we sin?"

In order to answer this question, we first need to distinguish between punishment and discipline. For believers in Jesus, all our sin – past, present and future – has already been punished on the cross. As Christians, we will never be punished for sin. That was done once for all. *"There is now no condemnation for those who are in Christ Jesus" (Romans 8:1).* Because of the sacrifice of Christ, God sees only the righteousness of Christ when He looks at us. Our sin has been nailed to the cross with Jesus, and we will never be punished for it.

The sin that remains in our lives, however, does sometimes require God's discipline. If we continue to act in sinful ways and we do not repent and turn from that sin, God brings His divine discipline to bear upon us. If He did not, He would not be a loving and concerned Father. Just as we discipline our own children for their welfare, so does our heavenly Father lovingly correct His children for their benefit. *Hebrews 12:7-13 tells us, "As you endure this divine discipline, remember that God is treating you as his own children. Whoever heard of a child who was never disciplined? If God doesn't discipline you as he does all of his children, it means that you are illegitimate and are not really his children after all. Since we respect our earthly fathers who disciplined us, should we not all the more cheerfully submit to the discipline of our heavenly Father and live forever? For our earthly fathers disciplined us for a few years, doing the best they knew how. But God's discipline is always right and good for us because it means we will share in his holiness. No discipline is enjoyable while it is happening--it is painful! But afterward there will be a quiet harvest of right living for those who are trained in this way."*

Discipline, then, is how God lovingly turns His children from rebellion to obedience. Through discipline our eyes are opened more clearly to God's perspective on our lives. As King David stated in *Psalm 32*, discipline causes us to confess and repent of sin we have not yet dealt with. In this way discipline is cleansing. It is also a growth catalyst. The more we know about God, the more we know about His desires for our lives. Discipline presents us with the opportunity to learn and to conform ourselves to the image of Christ *(Romans 12:1-2)*. Discipline is a good thing!

We need to remember that sin is a constant in our lives while we are yet on this earth *(Romans 3:10, 23)*. And as such, we not only have to deal with God's discipline for our disobedience, but we also have to deal with the natural consequences resulting from sin. If a believer steals something, God will forgive him and cleanse him from the sin of theft, restoring fellowship between Himself and the repentant thief. However, the societal consequences of theft can be severe, resulting in fines or even jail time. These are natural consequences of sin and must be endured. But God works even through those to increase our faith and glorify Himself.

21. Question: "Why is God a jealous God?"

It is important here to understand how the word jealous is used. How it used in *Exodus 20:5* to describe God is different from how it is used to describe the sin of jealousy *(Galatians 5:20)*. When we use the word jealous, we use it in the sense of being envious of someone who has something we don't have. A person might be jealous or envious of another person because he or she has a nice car or home *(possessions)*. Or a person might be jealous or envious of another person because of some ability or skill that other person has *(such as athletic ability)*. Another example would be that one person might be jealous or envious of another because of his or her beauty.

When we look at this verse, we find that it is not that God is jealous or envious because someone has something He wants that He does not possess. *Exodus 20:4-5 says, "You shall not make for yourself a carved image, or any likeness of anything that is in heaven above, or that is in the earth beneath, or that is in the water under the earth; you shall not bow down to them nor serve them. For I, the LORD your God, am a jealous God..."* Notice that in this verse God is talking about being jealous if someone gives something that belongs to Him to another.

In these verses, God is speaking of people making idols and bowing down and worshiping those idols instead of giving God the worship that belongs to Him alone. God is possessive of the worship and service that belong to Him. It is a sin (as God points out in this commandment) to worship or serve anything other than Him. So, in summary, it is a sin when we desire, or we are envious, or we are jealous of someone because he has something that we do not have. It is a different use of the word jealous when God says He is jealous. What He is jealous for belongs to Him; worship and service belong to Him alone, and are to be given to Him alone.

Perhaps a practical example will help us to understand the difference. If a husband sees another man flirting with his wife, he is right to be jealous, for only he has the right to flirt with his wife. This type of jealousy is not sinful. Rather, it is entirely appropriate. Being jealous for something that belongs to you is good and appropriate. Jealousy is a sin when it is a desire for something that does not belong to you. Worship, praise, honor, and adoration belong to God alone, for only He is truly worthy of it. Therefore, God is rightly jealous when worship, praise, honor, or adoration is given to idols. This is precisely the jealousy the Apostle Paul described in *2 Corinthians 11:2, "I am jealous for you with a godly jealousy..."*

22. Question: "Who created God? Where did God come from?"

The atheist Bertrand Russell wrote in his book *"Why I am Not a Christian"* that if it is true that all things need a cause then God must also need a cause. He concluded from this that if God needed a cause then God was not God (and if God is not God then of course there is no God). This was basically a slightly more sophisticated form of the childlike question, "Who made God?" Even a child knows that things do not come from nothing, so if God is a "something" then He must have a cause as well, right?

The question is tricky because it sneaks in the false assumption that God came from somewhere and then asks where that might be. The answer is that the question does not even make sense. It is like asking, "What does blue smell like?" Blue is not in the category of things that have odor, so the question itself is flawed. In the same way, God is not in the category of things that are created, or come into existence, or are caused. God is uncaused and uncreated - He simply exists.

How do we know this? Well, we know that from nothing, nothing comes. So if there was ever a time when there was absolutely nothing in existence then nothing would have ever come to exist. But things do exist. Therefore, since there could never have been absolutely nothing, something had to have always been existing. That ever-existing thing is what we call God.

23. Question: "How do I get the image of God as imposing and angry out of my mind?"

Perhaps it will help to consider one of the most profound statements in the Bible: "God is love" (1 John 4:8). Never was a more important declaration made than this; never was more meaning crowded into a few words than in this short sentence—God is love. This is a profound statement. God doesn't just love; He is love. His nature and essence are love. Love permeates His very being and infuses all His other attributes, even His wrath and anger. When we see God as angry, it might help to realize that His anger is filtered through His great love.

It might also help to understand that God is never angry with His children, those who have come to Christ in faith for forgiveness of sin. All His anger was directed against His own Son on the cross, and He will never again be angry with those for whom Christ died. The Bible tells us that "God is angry with the wicked every day" (Psalm 7:11), but we who belong to Christ are not "the wicked." We are perfect in God's sight, because when He looks at us, He sees Jesus. "For He has made Him who knew no sin, to be sin for us, that we might become the righteousness of God in Him" (2 Corinthians 5:21). All God's wrath against our sin was poured out on Jesus on the cross, and He simply will not be angry with us ever again if we have placed our faith in Christ. He did this out of His great love for His own.

The fact that God is loving does not cancel out His holy requirement of perfection. However, because He is loving, He sent Christ to die on the cross in our place, and this completely satisfies God's requirement of perfection. Because He is loving, God provided a way for man to be no longer separated from Him by sin, but to be able to enter into a relationship with Him as a welcome part of God's family, placed in that family because of the finished work of Christ on the cross (John 1:12; 5:24).

If, even knowing these things, we still see God as angry and imposing, it could be that we are not sure of our own relationship to Him. The Bible encourages us to "examine yourselves, whether you are in the faith" (2 Corinthians 13:5). If we doubt that we truly belong to Christ, we only need to repent and ask Him into our hearts. He will forgive us our sin and give us His Holy Spirit who will live in our hearts and assure us that we are His children. Once we are assured that we are His, we can draw close to Him by reading and studying His Word and by asking Him to show Himself to us as He truly is. God loves each of us and desires to know us in a personal relationship. He has assured us that if we seek Him with all our hearts, we will surely find Him (Jeremiah 29:13). Then we will truly know Him, not as imposing and angry, but as a loving and gracious Father.

24. Question: "Does God change His mind?"

Malachi 3:6 declares, *"I the LORD do not change. So you, O descendants of Jacob, are not destroyed."* Similarly, *James 1:17* tells us, *"Every good and perfect gift is from above, coming down from the Father of the heavenly lights, who does not change like shifting shadows."* The meaning of *Numbers 23:19* could not be more clear, *"God is not a man, that He should lie, nor a son of man, that He should change His mind. Does He speak and then not act? Does He promise and not fulfill?"* No, God does not change His mind. These verses assert that God is unchanging, and unchangeable.

However, this appears to contradict what is taught in other verses, such as *Genesis 6:6, "The LORD was grieved that He had made man on the earth, and His heart was filled with pain."* Also, *Jonah 3:10* which says, *"When God saw what they did and how they turned from their evil ways, He had compassion and did not bring upon them the destruction He had threatened."* Similarly, *Exodus 32:14* proclaims, *"Then the LORD relented and did not bring on His people the disaster He had threatened."* These verses speak of the Lord "repenting" of something, and seem to be contrary to verses that teach that God is unchanging. However, close examination of these passages reveals that these are not truly indications that God is capable of changing. In the original language, the word that is translated as "repent," or "relent," is the Hebrew expression of "to be sorry for." Being sorry for something does not mean that a change has occurred; it simply means that there is regret for something that has taken place.

Consider in *Genesis 6:6* that "*...The LORD was grieved that He had made man on the earth.*" This verse even goes on to say "*...His heart was filled with pain.*" This verse declares that God had regret for creating man. However, obviously He did not reverse His decision. Instead, through Noah, He allowed man to continue to exist. The fact that we are alive today is living proof that God did not change His mind about creating man. Also, the context of this passage is a description of the sinful state man was living in, and it is man's sinfulness that triggered God's sorrow, not man's existence. Consider what *Jonah 3:10* says: "*...He had compassion and did not bring upon them the destruction He had threatened.*" Again, the same Hebrew word is used here, which expresses "to be sorry for." Why was God "sorry" for what He had planned for the Ninevites? Because they had a change in heart, and as a result, changed their ways from disobedience to obedience. God is entirely consistent. God was going to judge Nineveh because of its evil. However, Nineveh repented and changed its ways. As a result, God had mercy on Nineveh, which is entirely consistent with His character.

Romans 3:23 teaches us that all men sin, and fall short of God's standard. *Romans 6:23* states that the consequence for this is death (spiritual and physical). So, the people of Nineveh were deserving of punishment. All of us face this same situation, as it is man's choice to sin that separates us all from God. Man cannot hold God responsible for his own predicament. So it would be contrary to the character of God to not punish the Ninevites had they continued in sin. However, the people of Nineveh turned to obedience, and for that the Lord chose not to punish them as He had originally intended. Did the change on the part of the Ninevites obligate God to do what he did? Absolutely not! God cannot be placed in a position of obligation to man. God is good and righteous, and chose not to punish the Ninevites as a result of their change of heart. If anything, what this passage does is point to the fact that God does not change, because had the Lord not preserved the Ninevites, this would be contrary to the character of God.

The Scriptures that describe God apparently "changing His mind" are human attempts to explain the actions of God. God was going to do something, but instead did something else. To us, that sounds like a change. But to God, who is omniscient and sovereign, it is not a change. God always knew what He was going to do. God also knew what He needed to do to cause humanity to do what He wanted them to do. God threatened Nineveh with destruction, knowing that it would cause Nineveh to repent. God threatened Israel with destruction, knowing that Moses would intercede. God does not regret His decisions, but is saddened by some of what humanity does in response to His decisions. God does not change His mind, but rather acts consistently to His Word in response to our actions.

25. Question: "Has anyone ever seen God?"

The Bible tells us that no one has ever seen God *(John 1:18)* except the Lord Jesus Christ. In *Exodus 33:20*, God declares, *"You cannot see My face, for no one may see Me and live."* These Scriptures seem to contradict other Scriptures which describe various people "seeing" God. For example, *Exodus 33:19-23* describes Moses speaking to God, "face to face." How could Moses speak with God "face to face" if no one can see God's face and live? In this instance, the phrase "face to face" is a figure of speech indicating they were in very close communion. God and Moses were speaking to each other "as if" they were two human beings having a close conversation.

In *Genesis 32:30*, Jacob saw God appearing as an angel – he did not truly see God. Samson's parents were terrified when they realized they had seen God *(Judges 13:22)*, but they had only seen Him appearing as an angel. Jesus was God in the flesh *(John 1:14)* so when people saw Him, they were seeing God. So, yes, God can be "seen" and many people have "seen" God. At the same time, no one has ever seen God revealed in all His glory. In our fallen human condition, if God were to fully reveal Himself to us, we would be consumed. Therefore, God veils Himself and appears in forms in which we can "see" Him. However, this is different than seeing God with all His glory and holiness displayed. People have seen visions of God, images of God, and appearances of God – but no one has ever seen God in all His fullness *(Exodus 33:20)*.

26. Question: "What does it mean to have the fear of God?"

For the unbeliever, the fear of God is to fear the judgment of God and eternal death, which is eternal separation from God *(Luke 12:5; Hebrews 10:31)*. For the believer, the fear of God is something much different. The believer's fear is reverence of God. *Hebrews 12:28-29* is a good description of this, *"Therefore, since we receive a kingdom which cannot be shaken, let us show gratitude, by which we may offer to God an acceptable service with reverence and awe; for our God is a consuming fire."* This reverence and awe is exactly what the fear of God means for Christians. This is the motivating factor for us to surrender to the Creator of the Universe.

Proverbs 1:7 declares, *"The fear of the LORD is the beginning of knowledge..."* Until we understand who God is, and develop a reverential fear of Him, we cannot have true wisdom. True wisdom comes only from understanding who God is – that He is holy, just, and righteous. *Deuteronomy 10:12,20 & 21* records, *"Now, Israel, what does the LORD your God require from you, but to fear the LORD your God, to walk in all His ways and love Him, and to serve the LORD your God with all your heart and with all your soul, You shall fear the LORD your God; you shall serve Him and cling to Him, and you shall swear by His name. He is your praise and He is your God, who has done these great and awesome things for you which your eyes have seen."* The fear of God is the basis for our walking in His ways, serving Him, and yes, loving Him.

Many have the tendency of minimizing the fear of God for believers to "respecting" Him. While respect is definitely included in the concept of fearing God, there is more to it than that. A Biblical fear of God, for the believer, includes understanding how much God hates sin, and fearing His judgment on sin – even in the life of a believer. *Hebrews 12:5-11* describes God's discipline of the believer. While it is done in love *(Hebrews 12:6)*, it is still a fearful thing. As children, the fear of discipline from our parents prevented, hopefully, some evil actions. The same should be true in our relationship with God. We should fear His discipline, and therefore, seek to live our lives in such a way that pleases Him.

Believers are not to be "scared" of God. We have no reason to be scared of Him. We have His promise that nothing can separate us from His love *(Romans 8:38-39)*. We have His promise that He will never leave us or forsake us *(Hebrews 13:5)*. Fearing God means having such a reverence for Him, that it has a great impact on the way we live our lives. The fear of God is respecting Him, submitting to His discipline, and worshipping Him in awe.

27. Question: "Is it wrong to question God?"

At issue is not whether we should question God, but in what manner - and for what reason - we question Him. To question God is not in itself wrong. The prophet Habakkuk had questions for God concerning the timing and agency of the Lord's plan. Habakkuk, rather than being rebuked for his questions, is patiently answered, and the prophet ends his book with a song of praise to the Lord. Many questions are put to God in the Psalms *(Psalms 10, 44, 74, 77)*. These are the cries of the persecuted, which are desperate for God's intervention and salvation. Although God does not always answer our questions in the way we want, we conclude from these passages that a sincere question from an earnest heart is welcomed by God.

Insincere questions, or questions from a hypocritical heart, are a different matter. *"He that cometh to God must believe that He is, and that He is a rewarder of them that diligently seek Him" (Hebrews 11:6)*. After King Saul had disobeyed God, his questions went unanswered *(1 Samuel 28:6)*. It is entirely different to wonder why God allowed a certain event than it is to directly question God's goodness. Having doubts is different from questioning God's sovereignty and attacking His character. In short, an honest question is not a sin, but a bitter, untrusting, or rebellious heart is. God is not intimidated by questions. God invites us to enjoy close fellowship with Him. When we "question

God," it should be from a humble spirit and open mind. We can question God, but we should not expect an answer unless we are genuinely interested in His answer. God knows our hearts, and knows whether we are genuinely seeking Him to enlighten us. Our heart attitude is what determines whether it is right or wrong to question God.

28. Question: "Is there anything God cannot do?"

On a clear night, look up at the stars in the sky. *Genesis 1* records that God made all of them! Imagine the power in just one star! But it is not just about raw power. There is intelligence and design packed in our universe down to the smallest DNA strand, down to the smallest sub-atomic particle. God's power and wisdom are beyond our comprehension. That is why the LORD said to Abraham in *Genesis 18:14, "Is anything too hard for the LORD?"* That is why the LORD said to Moses when Moses questioned how God could possibly supply meat to several million Israelites in the wilderness, *"Is the Lord's arm too short?" (Numbers 11:23).* That is why Jonathan told his armor bearer that the LORD didn't need a lot of soldiers to get a victory *(1 Samuel 14:6).*

Jeremiah 32:17 states, *"Ah Lord GOD! behold, thou hast made the heaven and the earth by thy great power and stretched out arm, and there is nothing too hard for thee."* Even in the spiritual realm, those that seem the farthest from salvation are not impossible for Him to reach *(Mark 10:25-27).* And as great as His power is, His love and mercy are just as great...even to the point of His willingness to send His own Son to die on the cross of Calvary to pay the penalty for a sinful mankind. He did this so that He, in complete justice, could forgive those who will turn away from self-reliance and sin to reliance upon Christ and His finished work. As parents, it would be far worse to see our children endure torment than go through it ourselves, and yet that is just what God the Father did. *John 3:16*, a familiar verse, states God's great love: *"For God so loved the world, that he gave his only begotten Son, that whosoever believeth in him should not perish, but have everlasting life."* This love was not just for the "good" people (there are none), but for us...a fallen, sinful, unlovely, rebellious people

(Romans 3:10-23)...and yet He chose to shower us with His love *(Romans 5:6-10)* when we didn't deserve it.

The only thing that God cannot do is act contrary to His own character and nature. For example, *Titus 1:2* states that He cannot lie. Because He is holy, He cannot sin *(Isaiah 6:3; 1 Peter 1:16)*. Because He is just, He cannot merely overlook sin. Because Christ paid the penalty for sin, He is now able to forgive those who will turn to Christ *(Isaiah 53:1-12; Romans 3:26)*.

Truly our God is an awesome God...unchanging, eternal, unlimited in power, in majesty, in knowledge, in wisdom, in love, in mercy, and in holiness. But we are very much like the Israelites who, even after seeing God display His power and love repeatedly, doubted both His love and power as they came face to face with each new trial in their lives *(e.g., Numbers 13-14)*. May God help us to honor Him with dependence and trust in Him through the next "crisis" we face, for He is a *"very present help in trouble" (Psalm 46:1)*.

29. Question: "Does God have a sense of humor?"

Perhaps the best indication that God does have a sense of humor is that He created man in His image *(Genesis 1:27)*, and certainly people are able to perceive and express humor. The American Heritage Dictionary defines a "sense of humor" as "...The ability to perceive, enjoy, or express what is comical or funny." According to this definition, then, God must show an ability to perceive, enjoy, or express what is comical. The difficulty is that people perceive what is comical differently, and what sinful man perceives as funny would not amuse a holy and perfect God. Much of what the world calls humor is not funny but is crass and crude and should have no part in a Christian's life *(Colossians 3:8)*. Other humor is expressed at the expense of others (tearing down rather than building up), again something contrary to God's Word *(Colossians 4:6; Ephesians 4:29)*.

An example of God's humor is the instance in which the Israelites were using the Ark of the Covenant like a good-luck charm in taking it to battle, and the Philistines ended up capturing it and placing it in their temple before their idol of Dagon. They came into the temple the next day and found Dagon flat on his face before the ark. They set him back up. The next morning, there he was again, but this time he had his hands and head cut off as a symbol of his powerlessness before the God of the ark *(1 Samuel 5:1-5)*. God's putting Dagon in a position of submission to His ark is a comical picture.

This incident is an example of God laughing at the foolishness of those who would oppose Him. *"See what they spew from their mouths - they spew out swords from their lips, and they say, 'Who can hear us?' But you, O LORD, laugh at them; you scoff at all those nations" (Psalm 59:7-9). Psalm 2:4* also reveals God laughing at those who would rebel against His kingship. It is like the comical picture of a kindergarten-aged child being upset at his parents and running away from home...all the way to his neighbor's house. But there is obviously a serious side to this as well, and although the picture of weak and silly man trying to match wits with an almighty and all-knowing God is comical, God takes no delight in their waywardness and its consequences but rather desires to see them turn around *(Ezekiel 33:11; Matthew 23:37-38)*.

A person does not crack jokes in the presence of one who has just lost a close loved one; silly jokes are out of place on such occasions. In the same way, God is focused on the lost and is looking for those who will care for their souls as He does. That is why our lives (while having times of refreshing and humor) are to be characterized by "soberness" (seriousness about making our lives count for Christ) *(1 Thessalonians 5:6,8; Titus 2:2,6)*.

30. Question: "Why is God so different in the Old Testament than He is in the New Testament?"

At the very heart of this question lies a fundamental misunderstanding of what both the Old and New Testaments reveal about the nature of God. Another way of expressing this same basic thought is when people say: "The God of the Old Testament is a God of wrath while the God of the New Testament is a God of love." The fact that the Bible is

God's progressive revelation of Himself to us through historical events and through His relationship with people throughout history might contribute to people's misconceptions about what God is like in the Old Testament as compared to the New Testament. However, when one reads both the Old and the New Testaments it quickly becomes evident that God is not different from one Testament to another and that God's wrath and His love are revealed in both Testaments.

For example, throughout the Old Testament, God is declared to be *"merciful and gracious, slow to anger and abundant in loving-kindness and truth" (Exodus 34:6; Numbers 14:18; Deuteronomy 4:31; Nehemiah 9:17; Psalm 86:5; Psalm 86:15; Psalm 108:4; Psalm 145:8; Joel 2:13)*. Yet in the New Testament, God's loving-kindness and mercy are manifested even more fully through the fact that *"For God so loved the world that He gave His only begotten Son, that whoever believes in Him should not perish but have everlasting life" (John 3:16)*. Throughout the Old Testament, we also see God dealing with Israel much the same way a loving father deals with a child. When they willfully sinned against Him and began to worship idols, God would chastise them, yet each and every time He would deliver them once they had repented of their idolatry. This is much the same way that we see God dealing with Christians in the New Testament. For example, *Hebrews 12:6* tells us that *"For whom the Lord loves He chastens, and scourges every son whom He receives."*

In a similar way, throughout the Old Testament we see God's judgment and wrath poured out on unrepentant sinners. Likewise, in the New Testament, we see that the wrath of God is still *"revealed from heaven against all ungodliness and unrighteousness of men who suppress the truth in unrighteousness" (Romans 1:18)*. Even with just a quick reading of the New Testament, it quickly becomes evident that Jesus talks more about hell than He does heaven. So, clearly, God is not any different in the Old Testament than He is in the New Testament. God by His very nature is immutable (unchanging). While we might see one aspect of His nature revealed in certain passages of Scripture more than other aspects, He Himself does not change.

When one really begins to read and study the Bible, it becomes clear that God is not any different from the Old Testament to the New Testament. Even though the Bible is really sixty-six individual books, written on two (or possibly three) continents, in three different languages, over a period of approximately 1500 years, by more than 40 authors (who came from many walks of life), it remains one unified book from beginning to end without contradiction. In it we see how a loving, merciful, and just God deals with sinful men in all kinds of situations. Truly, the Bible is God's love letter to mankind. God's love for His creation, especially for mankind, is evident all through Scripture. Throughout the Bible we see God lovingly and mercifully calling people into a special relationship with Himself, not because they deserve it but because He is a gracious and merciful God, slow to anger and abundant in loving-kindness and truth. Yet we also see a holy and righteous God Who is the judge of all those who disobey His word and refuse to worship Him, instead turning to worship gods of their own creation, worshiping idols and other gods instead of worshiping the one and only true God *(Romans 1)*.

Because of God's righteous and holy character, all sin past, present, and future must be judged. Yet God in His infinite love has provided a payment for sin and a way of reconciliation so that sinful men can escape His wrath. We see this wonderful truth in verses like *1 John 4:10 "In this is love, not that we have loved God but that he loved us and sent his Son to be the propitiation for our sins."* In the Old Testament, God provided a sacrificial system whereby atonement could be made for sin, but this sacrificial system was only temporary and merely looked forward to the coming of Jesus Christ who would die on the cross to make a real substitutionary atonement for sin. The Savior that was promised in the Old Testament is more fully revealed in the New Testament, and the ultimate expression of God's love, the sending of His son Jesus Christ, is revealed in all its glory. Both the Old and the New Testaments were given *"to make us wise unto salvation" (2 Timothy 3:15)*. When we study them more closely, it really is evident that God is no different in the New Testament than He was in the Old Testament.

31. Question: "Is God / the Bible sexist?"

Sexism is one gender, usually male, having dominance over the other gender, usually female. The Bible contains many references to women that, in our modern minds, sound discriminatory towards women. Does this mean that God, and therefore the Bible, is sexist? We have to remember that the Bible describing an action does not necessarily mean that the Bible is endorsing that action. The Bible describes men treating women as little more than property, but that does not mean the Bible indicates approval of that action. Even in the instances where the Bible is giving a command regarding the treatment of women, it is not necessarily an indication of God's ideal standard. The Bible is far more focused on reforming our souls than our societies. God knows that a changed heart will result in a changed behavior.

During the Old Testament, the whole world was a patriarchal society. That status of history is very clear - not only in Scripture but in the social rules that governed most societies in the world. By modern value systems and worldly human viewpoint, that is called "sexist." God ordained the order in society, not man, and He is the author of the establishment principles of authority. However, like everything else, fallen man has corrupted this order. That has resulted in the inequality of the standing of men and women throughout history. The exclusion and the discrimination that we find in our world is not new. It is the result of the fall of man and the introduction of sin - which is rebellion against God. Therefore, we can rightly say that the term and the practice of "sexism" is a result of - a product of - the sin of mankind. The progressive revelation of the Bible leads us to the cure for sexism, and indeed all of the sinful practices of the human race.

To find and maintain a spiritual balance between the God-ordained positions of authority, we must look to Scripture. The New Testament is the fulfillment of the Old, and in it we find principles that tell us the correct line of authority and the cure for sin, the ill of all mankind, and that includes discrimination based upon gender.

The cross of Christ is the great equalizer. *John 3:16 says*, *"Whosoever will,"* and that is an all-inclusive statement that leaves no one out on the basis of position in society, mental capacity, or gender. We also find a passage in *Galatians 3:26-28* that tells us of our equal opportunity for salvation. *"For we are all the children of God by faith in Jesus Christ. For as many of you as have been baptized (identified) into Christ have put on Christ. There is neither Jew nor Greek, there is neither bond nor free, there is neither male nor female; for ye are all one in Christ Jesus."* There is no sexism at the cross.

The Bible is not sexist. Why? Because it accurately portrays the results of sin. The Bible records all kinds of sin: slavery and bondage and the failures of its greatest heroes. Yet it also gives us the answer and the cure for those sins against God and His established order. That answer? It is a right relationship with God. The Old Testament was looking forward to the supreme sacrifice, and each time a sacrifice for sin was made, it was teaching the need for reconciliation to God. In the New Testament, the "Lamb that takes away the sin of the world" was born, died, was buried and rose again, and then ascended to His place in Heaven, and there He intercedes for us. It is through belief in Him that the cure for sin is found, and that includes the sin of sexism.

The charge of the sexism of the Bible is based upon a lack of knowledge of Scripture. When men and women of all ages have taken their God-ordained places and lived according to "Thus says the LORD," then there is a wonderful balance between the genders. That balance is what God began with, and it is what He will end with. There is an inordinate amount of attention paid to the various products of sin and not to the root of it. It is only when there is personal reconciliation with God through the LORD Jesus Christ that we find true equality. *"You shall know the truth, and the truth shall make you free" (John 8:32).*

It is also very important to understand that the Bible's ascribing different roles to men and women is not sexism. The Bible makes it abundantly clear that God expects men to take the leadership role in the church and the home. Does this make women inferior? Absolutely not. Does this mean women are less intelligent, less capable, or viewed as less in God's eyes? Absolutely not! What it means is that in our sin-stained world, there has to be structure and authority. God has instituted the roles of authority for our good. Sexism is the abuse of these roles…not the existence of these roles.

32. Question: "Why does God demand, seek, or request that we worship Him?"

What is worship? Worship means "to give honor, homage, reverence, respect, adoration, praise, or glory to a superior being." God demands worship because He and He alone is worthy of it. He is the only being that truly deserves worship. He requests that we acknowledge His greatness, His power and His glory. *Revelation 4:11* tells us, *"You are worthy, O Lord, to receive glory and honor and power; For You created all things, And by Your will they exist and were created."* God created us, and He is a God who will not be usurped. *"You shall not make for yourself a carved image - any likeness of anything that is in heaven above, or that is in the earth beneath, or that is in the water under the earth; you shall not bow down to them nor serve them. For I, the LORD your God, am a jealous God, visiting the iniquity of the fathers upon the children to the third and fourth generations of those who hate Me" (Exodus 10:3-5).* We must understand that God's jealousy is not the sinful envy that we experience, born out of pride. It is a holy and righteous jealousy that cannot allow the glory due only to Him to be given to another.

God expects us to worship Him as an expression of reverence and thanksgiving to Him. But God wants even more than that. God also expects us to be obedient to Him. He wants not only for us to love Him; He wants us to act justly towards each other, to show love and compassion to others. In this way, we present ourselves to Him as a living sacrifice, holy and pleasing to Him. This glorifies God and is our *"reasonable service" (Romans 12:1).* When we worship with an obedient heart and an open and repentant spirit, God is glorified, Christians are purified, the church is edified and the lost are evangelized. These are all the elements of true worship.

God also desires that we worship Him because our eternal destiny depends on our worship of the true and living God. *Philippians 3:3* describes the true church, the body of believers in Jesus Christ whose eternal destiny is heaven. *"For we are the circumcision, who worship God in the spirit, and rejoice in Christ Jesus, and have no confidence in the flesh."* In other words, the church is uniquely identified as God's people, but not through physical circumcision. The church is made up of those who worship God in their spirit rejoicing in Christ, and not trusting in themselves for salvation. Those who do not worship the true and living God are none of His, and their eternal destiny is hell. But the true worshippers are identified by their worship of God, and their eternal home is with the God they worship and adore.

God demands, seeks and requests our worship because He deserves it, because it is the nature of a Christian to worship Him, and because our eternal destiny depends upon it. That is the theme of redemptive history: to worship the true, living and glorious God.

33. Question: "Is God fair?"

Fortunately for us, God is not fair. Fairness would mean that everyone got exactly as he or she deserved and everyone would be treated the same. If God were completely fair, we would all spend eternity in hell paying for our sin, which is exactly what we deserve. We have all sinned against God *(Romans 3:23)* and are therefore worthy of eternal death *(Romans 6:23)*. If we received what we deserve, we would end up in the lake of fire *(Revelation 20:14-15)*. But God is not fair; instead, He is merciful and good, so He sent Jesus Christ to die on the cross in our place, taking the punishment that we deserve *(2 Corinthians 5:21)*. All we have to do is believe in Him and we will be saved, forgiven, and receive an eternal home in heaven *(John 3:16)*.

However, despite God's loving grace, no one would believe in Him on his own *(Romans 3:10-18)*. God has to draw us to Himself in order for us to believe *(John 6:44)*. God does not draw everyone, but only certain people He has sovereignly chosen *(Romans 8:29-30; Ephesians 1:5 & 11)*. This is not "fair" in our eyes because it appears God is not treating all people equally. However, God does not have to choose anyone. Those whom God has chosen are receiving God's love and grace. But all have the opportunity to respond to the revelation of the creation *(Psalm 19:1-3)*, as well as the conscience God has put within them *(Romans 2:15)*, and turn to God. Those who do not will receive what they truly deserve because of their rejection of Him. Those who reject Him receive the punishment they deserve *(John 3:18 & 36)*. Those who believe are receiving far more, and much better, than what they deserve. No one, though, is being punished beyond what he deserves. Is God fair? No. Thankfully, God is much more than fair! God is gracious, merciful, and forgiving - but also holy, just, and righteous.

34. Question: "Why did God command the extermination of the Canaanites, women and children included?"

In *1 Samuel 15:2 & 3*, God commanded Saul and the Israelites, *"This is what the LORD Almighty says: 'I will punish the Amalekites for what they did to Israel when they waylaid them as they came up from Egypt. Now go, attack the Amalekites and totally destroy everything that belongs to them. Do not spare them; put to death men and women, children and infants, cattle and sheep, camels and donkeys.'"* God ordered similar things when the Israelites were invading the Promised Land *(Deuteronomy 2:34; 3:6; 20:16-18)*. Why would God have the Israelites exterminate an entire group of people, women and children included?

This is honestly a very difficult issue. We do not fully understand why God would command such a thing, but at the same time we trust God that He is just – and recognize that we are incapable of fully understanding a sovereign, infinite, and eternal God. As we look at difficult issues such as this one, we have to remember that God's ways are higher than our ways and His thoughts are higher than our thoughts *(Isaiah 55:9; Romans 11:33-36)*. We have to be willing to trust God and have faith in Him even when we do not understand His ways.

Unlike us, God knows the future. God knew what the results would be if Israel did not completely eradicate the Amalekites. If Israel did not carry out God's orders, the Amalekites would come back to "haunt" the Israelites again and again. Saul claimed to have killed everyone but the Amalekite king Agag *(1 Samuel 15:20)*. Obviously Saul was lying…just a couple of decades later there were enough Amalekites to take David and his men's families captive *(1 Samuel 30:1-2)*. After David and his men attacked the Amalekites and rescued their families, 400 Amalekites escaped. If Saul had fulfilled what God had commanded him, this never would have occurred. Several hundred years later, a descendant of Agag, Haman, tried to have the entire Jewish people exterminated *(see the book of Esther)*. So, Saul's incomplete obedience almost resulted in Israel's destruction. God knew this would occur, so He ordered the extermination of the Amalekites ahead of time.

In regard to the Canaanites, God commanded, *"However, in the cities of the nations the LORD your God is giving you as an inheritance, do not leave alive anything that breathes. Completely destroy them - the*

Hittites, Amorites, Canaanites, Perizzites, Hivites and Jebusites - as the LORD your God has commanded you. Otherwise, they will teach you to follow all the detestable things they do in worshiping their gods, and you will sin against the LORD your God" (Deuteronomy 20:16-18). The Israelites failed in this mission as well, and exactly what God said would happen occurred *(Judges 2:1-3; 1 Kings 11:5; 14:24; 2 Kings 16:3 & 4)*. God did not order the extermination of these people to be cruel, but rather to prevent even greater evil from occurring in the future.

Probably the most difficult part of these commands from God is that God ordered the death of children and infants as well. Why would God order the death of innocent children?

⇒ Children are not innocent *(Psalm 51:5; 58:3)*.
⇒ These children would have likely grown up as adherents to the evil religions and practices of their parents.
⇒ By ending their lives as children, God enabled them to have entrance into Heaven. We strongly believe that all children who die are accepted into Heaven by the grace and mercy of God *(2 Samuel 12:22-23; Mark 10:14-15; Matthew 18:2-4)*.

Again, this answer does not completely deal with all the issues. Our focus should be on trusting God even when we do not understand His ways. We also have to remember that God looks at things from an eternal perspective, and that His ways are higher than our ways. God is just, righteous, holy, loving, merciful, and gracious. How His attributes work together can be a mystery to us – but that does not mean that He is not who the Bible proclaims Him to be.

35. Question: "Is God male or female?"

In examining Scripture, two facts become clear: First, that God is a Spirit, and does not possess human characteristics or limitations; second, that all the evidence contained in Scripture agrees that God revealed Himself to mankind in a male form. First of all, God's true nature needs to be understood. God is a person, obviously, because God exhibits all the characteristics of personhood: God has a mind, a will, an intellect, and emotions. God communicates, has relationships, and God's personal actions are evidenced throughout Scripture.

As *John 4:24* states, *"God is a Spirit: and they that worship Him must worship Him in spirit and in truth."* Since God is a spiritual being, God does not possess physical human characteristics. However, sometimes figurative language used in Scripture assigns human characteristics to God in order to make it possible for man to understand God. This assignment of human characteristics to describe God is called "anthropomorphism." Anthropomorphism is simply a means for God (a spiritual being) to communicate truth about His nature to mankind, a physical being. Since man is a physical being, man is limited in his understanding of those things beyond the physical realm, and anthropomorphism in Scripture helps man to understand who God is.

Some of the difficulty comes in examining the fact that man is created in God's image. *Genesis 1:26-27* says, *"And God said, Let us make man in our image, after our likeness: and let them have dominion over the fish of the sea, and over the fowl of the air, and over the cattle, and over all the earth, and over every creeping thing that creepeth upon the earth. So God created man in His [own] image, in the image of God created he Him; male and female created He them."*

What this means is that both man and woman are created in the image of God, in that they are greater than all the other creations as they, like God, have a mind, will, intellect, emotions, and moral capacity. Animals do not possess a moral capacity, and do not possess an immaterial component like mankind does. Genesis tells us that when man was created by God, God created man in His own image. The image of God is the spiritual component that man alone possesses. God created man to have a relationship with Him; man is the only creation designed for that purpose.

That said, man and woman are only patterned after the image of God - they are not tiny "carbon copies" of God, and the fact that there are men and women does not require that God have male and female features. Remember, being made in the image of God has nothing to do with physical characteristics.

We know that God is a spiritual being, and does not possess physical characteristics. This does not limit, however, how God may choose to reveal Himself to mankind. Scripture contains all the revelation God gave to man about Himself, and so is the only really objective source of information about God. In looking at what Scripture tells us, there are several observations of evidence about the form in which God revealed Himself to mankind:

To begin with, Scripture contains almost 170 references to God as the "Father." By necessity, one cannot be a father unless he is male. If God had chosen to be revealed to man in a female form, then the word "mother" would have occurred in these places, not "father." In the Old and New Testament both, masculine pronouns are used over and over again in reference to God.

Jesus Christ referred to God as the Father several times, and in other cases used masculine pronouns in reference to God. In the Gospels alone, Christ uses the term "Father" in direct reference to God nearly 160 times. Of particular interest is Christ's statement in *John 10:30*. He says here, *"I and [my] Father are one."* Obviously, Jesus Christ came in the form of a human man to die on the cross as payment for the sins of the world, and, like God the Father, was revealed to mankind in a male form. Scripture records numerous other instances where Christ utilized masculine nouns and pronouns in reference to God.

The New Testament Epistles (from Acts to Revelation) also contain nearly 900 verses where the word "theos"—a masculine noun in the Greek—is used in direct reference to God. In most cases, this is rendered "God" in English versions.

In countless references to God in Scripture, there is clearly a consistent pattern of His being referred to with masculine titles, nouns, and pronouns. While God is not a man, but is a Spirit, He chose a masculine form in order to reveal Himself to mankind. Likewise, Jesus Christ, who is constantly referred to with masculine titles, nouns, and pronouns, took a male form while He walked on the earth. The prophets of the Old Testament and the Apostles of the New Testament refer to both God and Jesus Christ with masculine names and titles. God chose to be revealed in this form in order for man to more easily grasp who God is. To assert that God chose a female form to be revealed to man is not consistent with the pattern established by Scripture. Again, had God chosen a feminine form, there would be more evidence in Scripture of that. That evidence simply does not exist. While God makes allowances in order to help mankind understand Him, it is important to not try to "force God into a box," so to speak, by placing limitations on Him that are not appropriate to the nature of who He is.

36. Question: "What is YHWH? What is the Tetragrammaton?"

The ancient Hebrew language that the Hebrew Scriptures were written in did not have vowels. In the original Hebrew, God's name is given as "YHWH." This is known as the Tetragrammaton. Because of the lack of vowels, Bible scholars debate how the Tetragrammaton "YHWH" was pronounced.

Contrary to what some Christians (and at least one cult that uses this name) believe, "Jehovah" is probably not the Divine Name revealed to Israel. Due to the Jewish fear of accidentally taking God's Name in vain *(Leviticus 24:16)*, they basically quit saying it out-loud altogether. Instead, when reading, they substituted the actual Tetragrammaton, which is only the consonants of the Divine Name "YHWH" since Hebrew is not usually written with vowels included, with the word Adonai (Lord). Even in the Septuagint, the Greek version of the Old Testament, the translators substituted Kurios (Lord) for the Divine Name. Eventually the vowels from Adonai ("Lord") or Elohim ("God") found their way into the consonants YHWH, thus forming "YaHWeH." But this does not mean that was how God's Name was originally pronounced.

Any number of vowel combinations are possible, and the Jews are as uncertain of the real pronunciation as are Christians. "Jehovah" is actually a much later (probably 16th century) variant in Latin. Here, the "Y" is substituted with a "J", Hebrew does not even have a "J" sound, and the "W" with a "V," plus another vowel combination, resulting in "JeHoVaH." This vowel combination is composed of the abbreviated forms of the imperfect, the participle, and the perfect of the Hebrew being verb (English "is") - thus the meaning of Jehovah could be said to be "he who will be, is, and has been."

So, what is God's name and what does it mean? The most likely choice for how the Tetragrammaton was pronounced is "Yahweh" or something very similar to that. The name "Yahweh" refers to God's self-existence. "Yahweh" is linked with how God described Himself in *Exodus 3:14, "God said to Moses, 'I AM WHO I AM.' This is what you are to say to the Israelites: 'I AM has sent me to you.'"* God's name is a reflection of His being. God is the only self-existent / self-sufficient being in the universe. Only God has life in and of Himself. That is the essential meaning of the Tetragrammaton / YHWH / Yahweh.

37. Question: "Does God make mistakes?"

Make no mistake about it, God makes no mistakes. *"Great is the LORD, and greatly to be praised; and His greatness is unsearchable" (Psalms 145:3)*. The original language for "unsearchable" incorporates the thought of not being possible to fathom or find out or enumerate. It is obvious that this statement cannot be made for one who could make a mistake, for then, even if only one mistake is made, it could be said that he were one who made at least one mistake; that is, his greatness could be quantified or enumerated as having been one who made one mistake, even if only one, and even if he were the only one who made only one.

"Great is our Lord, and of great power: His understanding is infinite" (Psalms 147:5). Again, the understanding of anyone capable of mistakes would be finite, not infinite. *"God is not a man, that He should lie; neither the son of man, that He should repent: hath He said, and shall He not do it? Or hath He spoken, and shall He not make it good?" (Numbers 23:19)*. Here we see that God is not like man who makes mistakes and has afterthoughts leading to a change of mind, or that makes decrees that he later has to annul because he has not considered all the consequences, or that he lacks the infinite power to bring to pass that which he has said. Also, He is not like man whose mistaken and sinful morality begs retribution. *"God is light, and in Him is no darkness at all" (1 John 1:5b). "The LORD is righteous in all His ways and holy in all his works" (Psalms 145:17)*.

Perhaps someone would feign to find God having second thoughts about something He had done in the scripture: *"And GOD saw that the wickedness of man was great in the earth, and that every imagination of the thoughts of his heart was only evil continually. And it repented the LORD that He had made man on the earth, and it grieved Him at His heart. And the LORD said, I will destroy man whom I have created from the face of the earth; both man, and beast, and the creeping thing, and the fowls of the air; for it repenteth me that I have made them" (Genesis 6:5-7).* First, note that He did not say He would destroy all men, for in the next verse, *"But Noah found grace in the eyes of the LORD" (Genesis 6:8).* And so it followed that Jesus came through Noah's son, Shem. No, God had not discovered a mistake in His works, not at all. He had a high and lofty purpose in permitting for a time the expression of the sin of mankind and angels.

To be sure, He made no mistake in creating Satan either, for, *"What if God, willing to show his wrath, and to make his power known, endured with much longsuffering the vessels of wrath fitted to destruction: And that he might make known the riches of his glory on the vessels of mercy, which he had afore prepared unto glory, Even us, whom he hath called, not of the Jews only, but also of the Gentiles?" (Romans 9:22-24). "And to make all men see what is the fellowship of the mystery, which from the beginning of the world hath been hid in God, who created all things by Jesus Christ: To the intent that now unto the principalities and powers in heavenly places might be known by the church the manifold wisdom of God, According to the eternal purpose which He purposed in Christ Jesus our Lord" (Ephesians 3:9-11).*

You see, God made no mistake, but had a purpose in all of this and the outcome is no surprise to Him, for He declares the end from the beginning, *"Remember the former things of old: for I am God, and there is none else; I am God, and there is none like me, Declaring the end from the beginning, and from ancient times the things that are not yet done, saying, My counsel shall stand, and I will do all my pleasure" (Isaiah 46:9-10).*

A word about the word "repent" as used in scripture. This is important. When used of God, it incorporates according to original language the thought of grief, even compassionate grief, and consolation or comfort, and action taken thereupon. Yes, God felt suffering and grief on our behalf, but that is not a sign of weakness or error, or regret of mistake. Rather, it is a sign of strength, of love on behalf of another; yes, of Agape love. In a word, it portrays specific action taken by God to counteract our mistakes; that is, our sins. *"But where sin abounded, grace did much more abound" (Romans 5:20b)*. When used of man, however, the word describes a change of heart, of thought and life's direction, based necessarily on the recognition of his own shortcomings, his sin, in the light of God's gracious call for his repentance for his own good.

Perhaps one may seem to think God has made a mistake in his or her own personal life's experiences. However, we are told, *"... we know that all things work together for good to them that love God, to them who are the called according to His purpose" (Romans 8:28)*. In all this we must understand that the things of this life are expendable and are being spent for our eternal reward according to His grace who, *"... is able to keep you from falling, and to present you faultless before the presence of His glory with exceeding joy" (Jude 1:24)*. *"For our light affliction, which is but for a moment, worketh for us a far more exceeding and eternal weight of glory; While we look not at the things which are seen, but at the things which are not seen: for the things which are seen are temporal; but the things which are not seen are eternal" (2 Corinthians 4:17-18)*. I am so glad my Lord and my God makes no mistakes with my life.

There is no fault in our God; there are no mistakes He has made. There is no fault, no mistakes made by His Son. In all of Satan's desperate effort to disclose one single fault in Jesus, he utterly failed while even his stooge Pontius Pilate declared, *"Then said Pilate to the chief priests and to the people, I find no fault in this man" (Luke 23:4)*.

This has been a very short discourse which could go on forever, for we serve an infallible God whose greatness cannot be enumerated. *"Many, O LORD my God, are thy wonderful works which thou hast done, and thy thoughts which are to us-ward: they cannot be reckoned up in order unto thee: if I would declare and speak of them, they are more than can be numbered" (Psalms 40:5)*. *"Who can utter the mighty acts of the LORD? Who can shew forth all His praise?" (Psalms 106:2)*. Here again, in this rhetorical question the scripture challenges us, just dares us to even try to quantify or qualify the greatness of our God. Were we able to point out even one single mistake or fault of His we could put a qualifier on His greatness and this scripture could be repealed, but no worry, it stands forever. *"For ever, O LORD, thy word is settled in heaven" (Psalms 119:89)*.

38. Question: "What does God look like?"

God is a spirit *(John 4:24)*, and so His appearance is not like anything we can describe. *Exodus 33:20* tells us, *"But,"* he said, *"you cannot see my face, for no one may see me and live."* As sinful human beings, we are incapable of even seeing God in all His glory and living. His appearance is utterly unimaginable and too glorious to be safely perceived by sinful man.

The Bible describes God appearing to people on various occasions. These should not be understood as describing exactly what God looks like, but rather as God revealing Himself to us in a way that we can understand. Two passages that powerfully describe God's appearance are *Ezekiel 1:26-28* and *Revelation 1:14-16*.

Ezekiel 1:26-28, "Above the expanse over their heads was what looked like a throne of sapphire, and high above on the throne was a figure like that of a man. I saw that from what appeared to be his waist up he looked like glowing metal, as if full of fire, and that from there down he looked like fire; and brilliant light surrounded him. Like the appearance of a rainbow in the clouds on a rainy day, so was the radiance around him." Revelation 1:14-16, "His head and hair were white like wool, as white as snow, and his eyes were like blazing fire. His feet were like bronze glowing in a furnace, and his voice was like the sound of rushing waters. In his right hand he held seven stars, and out of his mouth came a sharp double-edged sword. His face was like the sun shining in all its brilliance."

These passages represent Ezekiel's and John's best attempts at describing the glory of God that they witnessed. They had to use symbolic language and similes to describe that for which human language has no words, i.e., "what appeared like," "like the appearance," "he looked like," etc. We do know that when we are in heaven, *"we shall see Him as He is" (1 John 3:3)*. Sin will be no more, and we will be able to perceive God in all His glory.

39. Question: "Why does God allow sickness?"

The issue of sickness is always a difficult one to deal with. The key is remembering that God's ways are higher than our ways *(Isaiah 55:9)*. When we are suffering with a sickness, disease, or injury, we usually focus solely on our own suffering. In the midst of a trial of sickness, it is very difficult to focus on what good God might bring about as a result. *Romans 8:28* reminds us that God can bring about good from any situation. Many people look back on times of sickness as times when they grew closer to God, learned to trust Him more, and/or learned how to truly value life. This is the perspective God has because He is sovereign and knows the end result.

This does not mean sickness is always from God or that God always inflicts us with sickness to teach us a spiritual lesson. In a world tainted by sin, sickness, disease, and death will always be with us. We are fallen beings, with physical bodies prone to disease and illness. Some sickness is simply a result of the natural course of things in this world. Sickness can also be the result of a demonic attack. The Bible describes several instances when physical suffering was caused by Satan and his demons *(Matthew 17:14-18; Luke 13:10-16)*. So, some sickness is not from God, but from Satan. Even in these instances, God is still in control. God sometimes allows sin and/or Satan to cause physical suffering. Even when sickness is not directly from God, He will still use it according to His perfect will.

It is undeniable, though, that God sometimes intentionally allows, or even causes sickness to accomplish His sovereign purposes. While sickness is not directly addressed in the passage, *Hebrews 12:5-11* describes God disciplining us to *"produce a harvest of righteousness"*. Sickness can be a means of God's loving discipline. It is difficult for us to comprehend why God would work in this manner. But, believing in the sovereignty of God, there is no other option than suffering being something God allows and/or causes.

The clearest example of this in Scripture is found is *Psalm 119*. Notice the progression through *verses 67, 71, and 75 - "Before I was afflicted I went astray, but now I obey your word...It was good for me to be afflicted so that I might learn your decrees...I know, O LORD, that your laws are righteous, and in faithfulness you have afflicted me."* The author of *Psalm 119* was looking at suffering from God's perspective. It was good for him to be afflicted. It was faithfulness that caused God to afflict him. The result of the affliction was so that he could learn God's decrees and obey His Word.

Again, sickness and suffering is never an easy thing to deal with. One thing is for sure, sickness should not cause us to lose faith in God. God is good, even when we are suffering. Even the ultimate of suffering--death--is an act of God's goodness. It is hard to imagine that anyone who is in Heaven as a result of sickness or suffering regrets what they went through in this life.

One final note...when people are suffering, it is our responsibility to minister to them, care for them, pray for them, and comfort them. When a person is suffering, it is not always appropriate to emphasize that God will bring good out of the suffering. Yes, that is the truth. However, in the midst of suffering, it is not always the best time to share that truth. Suffering people need our love and encouragement, not necessarily a reminder of sound Biblical theology.

40. Question: "What does it mean that God is love?"

What does it mean that God is love? First we will look at how God's Word, the Bible, describes "love," and then we will see a few ways that it applies to God. *"Love is patient. Love is kind. It does not want what belongs to others. It does not brag. It is not proud. It is not rude. It does not look out for its own interests. It does not easily become angry. It does not keep track of other people's wrongs. Love is not happy with evil; but it is full of joy when the truth is spoken. It always protects. It always trusts. It always hopes. It never gives up. Love never fails"* (1 Corinthians 13:4-8a).

This is God's description of love. This is what He is like, and Christians are to make this their goal, (although always in the process). The greatest expression of God's love is communicated to us in *John 3:16* and *Romans 5:8. "For God so loved the world, that He gave His only begotten Son, that whoever believes in Him (Jesus Christ), will not perish but have everlasting life." "God demonstrated His love for us, in that while we were still sinners, Christ died for us."* We can see from these verses that it is God's greatest desire that we join Him in His eternal home, heaven. He has made the way possible by paying the price for our sins. He loves us because He chose to as an act of His will. *"My heart is stirred inside me. It is filled with pity for you" (Hosea 11:8b).* Love forgives. *"If we admit we have sinned (specifics), He will forgive us our sins. He will forgive every wrong thing we have done. He will make us pure" (1 John 1:9).*

Love (God) does not force Himself on anyone. Those who come to Him do so in response to His love. Love (God) shows kindness to all. Love (Jesus) went about doing good to everyone without partiality. Love (Jesus) did not covet what others had, living a humble life without complaining. Love (Jesus) did not brag about who He was in the flesh, although He could have overpowered anyone He ever came in contact with. Love (God) does not demand obedience. God did not demand obedience from His Son, but rather, Jesus willingly obeyed His Father in heaven. *"They must learn that I do exactly what my Father has commanded me to do" (John 14:31).* Love (Jesus) was/is always looking out for the interests of others.

This short description of love reveals a selfless life, in contrast with the selfish life of the natural man. Amazingly, God has given those who receive His Son Jesus as their personal Savior from sin the ability to love as He does, through the power of the Holy Spirit *(see John 1:12; 1 John 3:1, 23, 24)*. What a challenge and privilege!

41. Question: "Why does God create people when He knows they are going to go to hell?"

Please understand that God does not cause anybody to go to hell. Rather, man chooses to go there on his own. You can see the progression of those who reject Christ in the first 3 chapters of the book of *Romans*. The wrath of God is revealed against the unrighteous because man rejects the Creator and worships the creation *(Romans 1:18-20)*. Men profess to be wise in their own eyes *(v. 22)* and exchange the glory of God for created things. These people then continue in a downward spiral of sin that is listed in *verses 28-31*, sins to which all of us can relate. Not only do they participate in these sins, but they also approve of those who do them *(v. 32)*. Not only do men have the creation of the world to see God's power, but they also have their consciences convicting them of their sin *(2:14-15)*. In the end, man is left without excuse that we deserve to die, and we stand condemned in front of God.

Jesus Christ came in the flesh so that *"you may believe that Jesus is the Christ, the Son of God; and that believing you may have life in His name" (John 20:30,31)*. This is another witness to God's existence and also stands to condemn those men who choose to reject Christ as the Son of God. Because Christ came to pay the price of sin, and He came to *"explain the Father" (John 1:18)*, man has no excuse for rejecting Him. Men choose to go to hell because they reject Christ, not because God causes them to go there. God has paid the price, revealed Himself to all, and now men are *"without excuse" (Romans 1:20)*. God allows people to be born to give them the opportunity to believe, but it is man's responsibility to make that choice. What kind of God would He be if He did not give man the opportunity to place his faith in the Lord?

This is still a very difficult concept to grasp. We can only cling to what we know about God's nature and character, trust that His sovereignty and mercy do not contradict one another, and believe that everything He does and/or allows will ultimately be for His glory. We submit ourselves to Him in worship and obedience and trust that He *"works all things according to the counsel of His will" (Ephesians 1:11)* and that His ways are perfect, even when we don't understand them. *"He is the Rock, his work is perfect: for all his ways are judgment: a God of truth and without iniquity, just and right is he" (Deuteronomy 32:4)*.

42. Question: "Why does God allow evil men like Hitler and Saddam to come into power?"

"Every person is to be in subjection to the governing authorities. For there is no authority except from God, and those which exist are established by God. Therefore, whoever resists authority has opposed the ordinance of God; and they who have opposed will receive condemna-

tion upon themselves. For rulers are not a cause of fear for good be-havior, but for evil. Do you want to have no fear of authority? Do what is good, and you will have praise from the same" (Romans 13:1-3). One thing that is important here is that the teaching of this portion of Scripture is not on the ruler but our reaction to whatever ruler is in power. Therefore our focus is not to contemplate why God does what He does but our reaction or behavior to whatever God's decision is.

An interesting thing is that the book of *Romans* was probably written about 56-57 AD. The Emperor or Ruler at that time in Rome was Nero, who ruled from AD 54-68. Nero was an evil ruler, and during that time it is told that there was a terrible fire in Rome that destroyed a big por-tion of the city. It is told that Nero himself started that fire so he could expand his building projects. The problem was that he had to put the blame on someone, and he decided to blame the Christians. This started one of the biggest persecutions in the history of the church. Therefore, when Paul wrote this portion of Scripture, he was aware of the evil ruler of Rome, yet he does not wonder why God would put him in power. In fact Paul never mentions Nero at all. This also began to spread Christianity. It seems that throughout history whenever evil rulers came to power the gospel would spread.

"Therefore, thus says the LORD of hosts, the God of Israel: 'Behold, I am going to punish the king of Babylon and his land, just as I punished the king of Assyria'" (Jeremiah 50:18). God at times has used evil rul-ers to bring judgment on His people, but many times those countries or rulers would overstep their bounds with God, as did Assyria and Baby-lon, then God would punish them. God, even though He allows evil rulers or kings, would always set boundaries for them. When they would overstep those bounds, they would be punished. The greatest punishment is eternity in hell, and both Hitler and Lenin, who abused the people of God, have been serving their punishment in hell for a long time.

God does not explain why He allows evil rulers in His program, but He does tell us how to respond to them. If we live right in their eyes, we will often live and prosper as Daniel and his friends. At the same time, Peter and Paul both suffered hard deaths at the hands of evil emperors. Persecution is a part of life, but God can use that for good, as in the spread of the gospel.

43. Question: "Does God tempt us to sin?"

In *Genesis 22:1*, the Hebrew word translated "tempted" is the word NACAH and it means to test, try, prove, tempt, assay, or put to the proof. Because it has so many possible synonyms, we must look to the context and compare it to other passages. As we read the account of the event, we note that God did not intend Abram to complete the sacrifice of his promised heir. However, Abram did not know that, and was willing to carry out God's orders, knowing that if God did require this, He was able to raise Isaac up from the dead *(Hebrews 11:17-19)*. This passage in Hebrews (written in Greek) is translated 'Abram was "tried"' instead of saying he was "tempted." So the conclusion is that in *Genesis 22:1*, the Hebrew word translated "tempt" has to do with testing or evaluating something.

James 1:13 gives a guiding principle: no one has the right to say that he has been tempted *"of God."* The word "of" is essential to our understanding this statement, because it indicates the origin of something. This is an important part; because that means temptations to sin do not originate with God. In that sense, James concludes: God cannot be tempted with evil, and God does not tempt anyone to sin.

Another important word in this discussion is found in *James 1:3—"My brethren, count it all joy when ye fall into various trials; Knowing that the testing of your faith produces patience."* The Greek word translated "trials" connotes trouble, or something that breaks the pattern of peace, comfort, joy and happiness in someone's life. The verb form of this word means "to put someone or something to the test," with the purpose of discovering that person's nature or that thing's quality. God brings such tests to prove – and increase – the strength and quality of one's faith and to demonstrate its validity *(v. 2-12)*. So according to James, when we face temptations, God's purpose for them is to prove our faith, and they produce character. That is a high, good, noble motive.

Are there temptations which are designed to make us fail? Yes, but they do not come from God—they come from Satan *(Matthew 4:1)*, his evil angels *(Ephesians 6:12)* or from ourselves *(Romans 13:14; Galatians 5:13)*. God allows us to experience them and they are allowed for our benefit. God told Abram to offer Isaac—the temptation was not intended to get Abram to sin, but to test and prove his faith.

44. Question: "What is deism? What do deists believe?"

Deism is essentially the view that God exists, but that He is not directly involved in the world. Deism pictures God as the great "clockmaker" who created the clock, wound it up, and let it go. A deist believes that God exists and created the world, but does not interfere with His creation. Deists deny the Trinity, the inspiration of the Bible, the deity of Christ, miracles, and any supernatural act of redemption or salvation. Deism pictures God as ambivalent, uncaring, and uninvolved.

Deism is most definitely not Biblical. The Bible is filled with accounts of the miraculous. The Bible is, in fact, entirely an account of God interfering in His creation. *Daniel 4:34 & 35* records, *"His dominion is an eternal dominion; His kingdom endures from generation to generation. All the peoples of the earth are regarded as nothing. He does as He pleases with the powers of heaven and the peoples of the earth. No one can hold back His hand or say to Him: 'What have you done?'"* The world, history, and humanity are *"clay"* in the hands of God. God forms them and shapes them as He sees fit *(Romans 9:19-21).* The ultimate act of God "interfering" with His creation is when He took on human flesh in the Person of Jesus Christ *(John 1:1,14; 10:30).* Jesus Christ, God in the flesh, died to redeem His creation from the sin it had brought upon itself *(Romans 5:8; 2 Corinthians 5:21).*

I can understand how deism could be considered a "logical" position. There are some things in the world that seem to point to God being inactive in the affairs of the world. Why does God allow bad things to happen? Why does God allow the innocent to suffer? Why does God allow evil men to come to power? An inactive God would seem to answer these dilemmas. However, the Bible does not present God as inactive or uncaring. The Bible presents God as sovereign and incomprehensible. It is impossible for us to fully understand God and His ways. *Romans 11:33 & 34* remind us, *"Oh, the depth of the riches of the wisdom and knowledge of God! How unsearchable His judgments, and His paths beyond tracing out! Who has known the mind of the Lord? Or who has been His counselor?"* In *Isaiah 55:9* God declares, *"As the heavens are higher than the earth, so are my ways higher than your ways and my thoughts than your thoughts."*

Our failure in understanding God and His ways should not cause us to doubt His existence (atheism and agnosticism) or to question His involvement in the world (deism). God does exist and is very active in the world. Everything that takes place is subject to His sovereignty and authority. Deism is most definitely not Biblical. A deistic view of God is simply a failure in attempting to explain the unexplainable.

45. Question: "Does God still speak to us today?"

The Bible records God speaking audibly to people many times (*Exodus 3:14; Joshua 1:1; Judges 6:18; 1 Samuel 3:11; 2 Samuel 2:1; Job 40:1; Isaiah 7:3; Jeremiah 1:7; Acts 8:26; 9:15* – this is just a small sampling). There is no Biblical reason why God could not or would not speak to a person audibly today. With the hundreds of times the Bible records God speaking, we have to remember that they occur over the course of 4000 years of human history. God speaking audibly is the exception, not the rule. Even in the Biblically recorded instances of God speaking, it is not always clear whether it was an audible voice, an inner voice, or a mental impression.

God does speak to people today. First, God speaks to us through His Word *(2 Timothy 3:16 & 17)*. *Isaiah 55:11* tells us, *"so is my word that goes out from my mouth: it will not return to me empty, but will accomplish what I desire and achieve the purpose for which I sent it."* The Bible records God's words to us in everything we need to know in order to be saved and live the Christian life. *2 Peter 1:3 & 4* declares, *"His divine power has given us everything we need for life and godliness through our knowledge of Him who called us by his own glory and goodness. Through these He has given us His very great and precious promises, so that through them you may participate in the divine nature and escape the corruption in the world caused by evil desires."*

Secondly, God speaks through impressions, events, and thoughts. God helps us to discern right from wrong through our consciences *(1 Timothy 1:5; 1 Peter 3:16)*. God is in the process of conforming our minds to think His thoughts *(Romans 12:2)*. God allows events to occur in our lives to direct us, change us, and help us to grow spiritually *(James 1:2 -5; Hebrews 12:5-11)*. *1 Peter 1:6 & 7* reminds us, *"In this you greatly rejoice, though now for a little while you may have had to suffer grief in all kinds of trials. These have come so that your faith – of greater worth than gold, which perishes even though refined by fire – may be proved genuine and may result in praise, glory and honor when Jesus Christ is revealed."*

Finally, yes, God likely does sometimes speak audibly to people. It is highly doubtful, though, that this occurs as often as some people claim it does. Again, even in the Bible, God speaking audibly is the exception, not the ordinary. If anyone claims that God has spoken to him/her, always compare what is said with what the Bible says. If God were to speak today, His words would be in full agreement with what He has said in the Bible. God does not contradict Himself. *2 Timothy 3:16 & 17* proclaims, *"All Scripture is God-breathed and is useful for teaching, rebuking, correcting and training in righteousness, so that the man of God may be thoroughly equipped for every good work."*

46. Question: "Why does God allow natural disasters, i.e. earthquakes, hurricanes, and tsunamis?"

Why does God allow earthquakes, tornados, hurricanes, tsunamis, typhoons, cyclones, mudslides, and other natural disasters? The late 2004 tsunami tragedy in Asia, Hurricane Katrina in 2005 in the southeastern United States, and the 2008 cyclone in Myanmar have many people questioning God's goodness. It is distressing that natural disasters are often termed "acts of God" while no "credit" is given to God for years, decades, or even centuries of peaceful weather. God created the whole universe and the laws of nature *(Genesis 1:1)*. Most natural disasters are a result of these laws at work. Hurricanes, typhoons, and tornados are the results of divergent weather patterns colliding. Earthquakes are the result of the earth's plate structure shifting. A tsunami is caused by an underwater earthquake.

The Bible proclaims that Jesus Christ holds all of nature together *(Colossians 1:16-17)*. Could God prevent natural disasters? Absolutely! Does God sometimes influence the weather? Yes, see *Deuteronomy 11:17* and *James 5:17*. Does God sometimes cause natural disasters as a judgment against sin? Yes, see *Numbers 16:30-34*. The book of *Revelation* describes many events which could definitely be described as natural disasters (*Revelation chapters 6, 8, and 16*). Is every natural disaster a punishment from God? Absolutely not.

In much the same way that God allows evil people to commit evil acts, God allows the earth to demonstrate the consequences sin has had on Creation. *Romans 8:19-21* tells us, *"The creation waits in eager expectation for the sons of God to be revealed. For the creation was subjected to frustration, not by its own choice, but by the will of the one who subjected it, in hope that the creation itself will be liberated from its bondage to decay and brought into the glorious freedom of the children of God."* The fall of humanity into sin had effects on everything, including the universe we inhabit. Everything in Creation is subject to "frustration" and "decay." Sin is the ultimate cause of natural disasters just as it is the cause of death, disease, and suffering.

So, we are back to where we began. We can understand why natural disasters occur. What we do not understand is why God allows them to occur. Why did God allow the tsunami to kill over 225,000 people in Asia? Why did God allow Hurricane Katrina to destroy the homes of hundreds of thousands of people? What we can know is this...God is good! There are many amazing miracles, in instances of natural disaster, that occurred - preventing an even greater loss of life. Natural disasters cause millions of people to reevaluate their priorities in life. Hundreds of millions of dollars in aid is sent to help the people that are suffering. Christian ministries have the opportunity to help, minister, counsel, pray - and lead people to saving faith in Christ! God can, and does, bring great good out of terrible tragedies *(Romans 8:28)*.

47. Question: "What was God doing before He created the universe?"

Our finite minds find it hard to comprehend that before the universe was created, God existed alone. We know from *John 1:1* that Jesus also existed: "In the beginning was the Word and the Word was with God, and the Word was God. The preincarnate Christ was intimately united with the Father, so as to partake of His glory and to be appropriately called by the name God. He has himself explained it in *John*

17:5: "And now Father, glorify Me with Yourself with the glory which I had with You before the world was."

We also know that the Holy Spirit was present before we were created. *Genesis 1:1* describes the Spirit *"hovering over the face"* of the dark and formless earth. So, before time even existed, God existed in three Persons: Father, Son and Holy Spirit. The Trinity existed in perfect harmony and flawlessness, having all they needed in one another. David said in *Psalms 16:11* that *"joy and pleasures forever more"* are in the presence of God. That means to be in the presence of God carries with it an overwhelming sense of joy, fulfillment, and pleasure. Before creation, God felt complete joy and fulfillment as He perfectly beheld and communed with Himself. God has and always will experience complete joy because He has complete and perfect knowledge of Himself.

So before He created the universe, God experienced absolute satisfaction in Himself. God dwelt joyfully alone in eternity as the Trinity. These three were together in fellowship with one another from all eternity. They loved each other. We know at some point they discussed the redemption of mankind *(Ephesians 1:4-5; 2 Timothy 1:9; John 17:24)*, but everything else lies in mystery.

48. Question: "What is the difference between God's sovereign will and God's perfect will?"

When speaking of God's will, many people see three different aspects of it being revealed in the Bible. The first aspect of it is known as God's decretive, sovereign, or hidden will. This is God's "ultimate" will. This facet of God's will comes out of the recognition of God's sovereignty and the other aspects of God's nature. This expression of God's will focuses on the fact that God sovereignly ordains everything that comes to pass. In other words, there is nothing that happens that is outside of God's sovereign will. This aspect of God's will is seen in verses like *Ephesians 1:11*; where it tells us that God is the one *"who works all things according to the counsel of His will"* and *Job 42:2, "I know that You can do everything, And that no purpose of Yours can be withheld from You."* This view of God's will is based on the fact that because God is sovereign, His will can never be frustrated. Nothing happens that is beyond His control.

This understanding of His sovereign will does not imply that God causes everything to happen. Rather, it acknowledges that because He is sovereign, He must at least permit or allow whatever happens to happen. This aspect of God's will acknowledges the fact that even when God passively permits things to happen, He must choose to permit them, because He always has the power and right to intervene. God can always decide to either permit or stop the actions and events of this world. Therefore, as He allows things to happen, He has "willed" them in this sense of the word.

While God's sovereign will is often hidden from us until after it comes to pass, there is another aspect of His will that is plain to us. That aspect is what is known as His perceptive or revealed will. As the name implies, this facet of God's will simply acknowledges that God has chosen to reveal some of what His will for us is in the Bible. The perceptive will of God is God's declared will concerning what we should or should not do. For example, because of the revealed will of God, we can know that it is God's will that we do not steal, that we love our enemies, that we repent of our sins, and that we be holy as He is holy. This expression of God's will is revealed both in His Word as well as in our conscience, through which God has written His moral law upon the hearts of all men. The laws of God, whether found in Scripture or in our hearts, are binding upon us. We are accountable when we disobey them.

Understanding this aspect of God's will acknowledges that while we have the power and ability to disobey God's commands, we do not have the right to do so. Therefore, there is no excuse for our sin, and we cannot claim that by choosing to sin we are simply fulfilling God's sovereign decree or will. Judas was fulfilling God's sovereign will in betraying Christ, just as the Romans who crucified Him were. That does not justify their sins. They were no less evil or treacherous, and they were held accountable for their rejection of Christ *(Acts 4:27-28)*. Even though in His sovereign will God allows or permits sin to happen, we are still accountable to Him for that sin.

The third aspect of God's will that we see in the Bible is God's permissive or perfect will. This facet of God's will describes God's attitude and defines what is pleasing to Him. For example, while it is clear that God takes no pleasure in the death of the wicked, it is also clear that He most surely wills or decrees their death. This expression of God's will is revealed in the many verses of Scripture which indicate what God does and does not take pleasure in. For example, in *1 Timothy 2:4* we see that God desires *"all men to be saved and to come to the knowledge of the truth,"* and yet we know that God's sovereign will is that *"no one can come to Me unless the Father who sent Me draws him; and I will raise him up at the last day" (John 6:44).*

If we are not careful, Christians can easily become preoccupied or even obsessed with finding the "will" of God for our lives. However, if the will we are seeking is His secret, hidden, or decretive will - we are on a foolish quest. God has not chosen to reveal that aspect of His will for us. What we should seek to know is the perceptive or revealed will of God. The true mark of spirituality is when people desire to know and live according to the will of God as revealed in the Scripture, and that can be summarized as *"be holy for I am Holy" (1 Peter 1:15-16).* Our responsibility is to obey the revealed will of God and not to speculate on what His hidden will for us might be. While we should seek to be *"led by the Holy Spirit,"* we must never forget that the Holy Spirit is primarily leading us to righteousness and to being conformed into the image of Christ so that our lives will glorify God. God calls us to live our lives by every word that proceeds from His mouth.

Living according to His revealed will should be the chief aim or purpose of our lives. *Romans 12:1 & 2* summarize this truth as we are called to present our *"bodies a living sacrifice, holy, acceptable to God, which is your reasonable service. And do not be conformed to this world, but be transformed by the renewing of your mind, that you may prove what is that good and acceptable and perfect will of God."* To know the will of God we should immerse ourselves in the written Word of God, saturating our minds with it, and praying that the Holy Spirit will transform us through the renewing of our minds, so that the result is what is good, acceptable and perfect - the will of God.

49. Question: "What is the immutability of God?"

The immutability of God (that He does not change) is clearly taught throughout Scripture in countless passages. For example, in *Malachi 3:6* God affirms, *"I the Lord do not change."* (See also *Numbers 23:19; 1 Samuel 15:29; Isaiah 46:9-11; Ezekiel 24:14.*) *James 1:17* tells us *"Every good gift and every perfect gift is from above and comes down from the Father of lights, with whom is no variableness nor shadow of turning."* The shadow of turning refers to the sun which eclipses, and turns, and casts its shadow. It rises and sets, appears and disappears every day; and it comes out of one tropic, and enters into another at certain seasons of the year. But with God, who is light itself, there is no darkness at all; there is no change, nor anything like it. He is unchangeable in His nature, perfections, purposes, promises, and gifts. He, being holy, cannot turn to that which is evil; nor can He, who is the fountain of light, be the cause of darkness, and since every good and perfect gift comes from Him, evil cannot proceed from him, nor can he tempt any to it. The Bible is very clear that God does not change, neither His mind, His will, nor His nature.

Seen from a logical viewpoint, there are several reasons why it is impossible for God to change. First, if anything changes it must do so in some chronological order. There must be a point in time before the change and a point in time after the change. Therefore, for change to take place it must happen within the constraints of time; however, God is eternal and exists outside of the constraints of time (*Psalm 33:11; Psalm 41:13; Psalm 90:2-4; John 17:5; 2 Timothy 1:9*).

Second, if anything changes it must change for the better or the worse, because a change that makes no difference is not a change. For change to take place, either something that is needed is added, which is a change for the better, or something that is needed is lost, which is a change for the worse. But since God is perfect, He does not need anything. Therefore, He cannot change for the better. If God were to lose something He would not be perfect; therefore, He cannot change for the worse.

Third, when someone changes his/her mind, it is often because new information has come to light that was not previously known, or the circumstances have changed that require a different kind of attitude or action. Because God is omniscient, He cannot learn something new that He did not already know. So, when the Bible speaks of God changing His mind, it must be understood that the circumstance or situation has changed, not God. So when *Exodus 32:14* and *1 Samuel 15:11-29* talk about God changing His mind, it is simply describing a change of dispensation, and outward dealings, toward man.

Numbers 23:19 is very clear, *"God is not a man, that He should lie, nor a son of man, that He should change His mind. Does He speak and then not act? Does He promise and not fulfill?"* No, God does not change His mind. These verses affirm the doctrine of God's immutability: He is unchanging and unchangeable.

50. Question: "Could God create a rock so heavy He could not lift it?"

This question is frequently asked by skeptics of God, the Bible, Christianity, etc. If God can create a rock that He cannot lift, then God is not omnipotent. If God cannot create a rock so heavy that He cannot lift it, then God is not omnipotent. According to this argument, omnipotence is self-contradictory. Therefore, God cannot be omnipotent. So, the question, could God create a rock so heavy He could not lift it? The quick answer is "No." But the explanation is far more important to understand than the answer...

This question is based on a popular misunderstanding about the definitions of words like "almighty" or "omnipotent." These terms do not mean that God can do anything. Rather, they describe the amount of God's power. Power is the ability to effect change - to make something happen. God (being unlimited) has unlimited power, and the Bible affirms this (*Job 11:7-11, 37:23; 2 Corinthians 6:18; Revelation 4:8*; etc.). Therefore, God can do whatever is possible to be done. God cannot, however, do that which is actually impossible. This is because true impossibility is not based on the amount of power one has, it is based on what is really possible. The truly impossible is not made possible by adding more power. Therefore, unless context indicates otherwise (e.g. *Matthew 19:26* where man's ability is being shown in contrast to God's), impossibility means the same thing whether or not God is involved.

So, the first part of the question is based on a false idea; that God, being almighty means that He can do anything. In fact, the Bible itself lists things God cannot do - like lie or deny Himself (*Hebrews 6:18; 2 Timothy 2:13; Titus 1:2*). The reason He cannot do these things is because of His nature and the nature of reality itself. God cannot do what is not actually possible to be done, like creating a two-sided triangle, or a married bachelor. Just because words can be strung together this way does not make the impossible possible - these things are contradictions, they are truly impossible in reality. Now, what about this rock? A rock would have to be infinitely large to defeat an infinite amount of lifting power. But an infinite rock is a contradiction since material objects cannot be infinite. Only God is infinite. There cannot be two infinites. So the question is actually asking if God can make a contradiction - which He cannot.

51. Question: "Why does God refer to Himself in the plural in *Genesis 1:26* and *3:22*?"

Genesis 1:26 says, *"Then God said, 'Let **us** make man in **our** image, in **our** likeness, and let them rule over the fish of the sea and the birds of the air, over the livestock, over all the earth, and over all the creatures that move along the ground.'"* *Genesis 3:22* states, *"And the LORD God said, 'The man has now become like one of us...'"* There are other Scriptures in the Old Testament that refer to God using the plural. It is also interesting to note that "Elohim," one of the primary titles of God in the Old Testament (occurring over 2500 times), is in the plural.

Some people have used these scriptures to hypothesize that there is more than one God. We can rule out polytheism (belief in multiple gods), because that would contradict countless other Scriptures that tell us that God is one and that there is only one God. Three times in *Isaiah 45* alone, He states: *"I am the LORD, and there is no other; there is no God besides Me" (v. 5,6 & 18)*. A second possible explanation is that God was referring to the angels by saying "us" and "our." However, the Bible nowhere states that angels have the same "image" or "likeness" as God (see *Genesis 1:26*). That description is given to humanity alone.

Since the Bible, and the New Testament especially, presents God as a Trinity (three Persons but only one God), *Genesis 1:26* and *3:22* can only represent a conversation within the Trinity. God the Father is having a "conversation" with God the Son and/or God the Holy Spirit. The Old Testament hints at the plurality of God, and the New Testament clarifies this plurality with the doctrine of the Trinity. Obviously, there is no way we can fully understand how this works – but God has given us enough information to know that He does exist in three Persons, - Father, Son and Holy Spirit.

52. Question: "Why does God require faith? Why doesn't God "prove" Himself to us so there is no need for faith?"

Our relationship with God is similar to our relationship with others in that all relationships require faith, and I can never and will never fully know any other person. This is because we are incapable of fully knowing others because we cannot experience all they experience nor enter into their minds to know what their thoughts and emotions are. *Proverbs 14:10* says, *"The heart knows its own bitterness, and a stranger does not share its joy."* We are even incapable of knowing our own heart fully. *Jeremiah 17:9* says that the human heart is wicked and deceptive, and this verse asks concerning the human heart, *"Who can know it?"* In other words, the human heart is such that it seeks to hide the depth of its wickedness and gloss over it, deceiving even its owner. We do this through blame shifting, justifying wrong behavior, minimizing our sins, etc.

Because we are incapable of fully knowing fellow humans, to some degree faith (trust) is an integral ingredient in all relationships. For example, my wife gets into a car with me driving, trusting me to drive safely, even though I drive faster than she does on winter roads. She and my children trust me to act in their best interest when handling finances or when I am away from them and can choose to act in faithfulness to them or not. We all share information about ourselves with others, trusting they won't betray us with that knowledge. We drive down the road, trusting those driving around us to follow the rule of the road. So, whether with strangers or with intimate friends and companions, because we cannot fully know others, trust is always a necessary component of our relationships.

If we cannot know our fellow finite human beings fully, how can we expect to fully know an infinite God? Even if He should desire to fully reveal Himself, it is impossible for us to fully know Him. It is like trying to pour the ocean (seemingly infinite in quantity) into a quart-measuring jar (finite)... impossible! But nonetheless, even as we can have meaningful relationships with those around us that we have grown to trust because of our knowledge of them and of their character, so God has revealed enough about Himself through His creation *(Romans 1:18-21)*, through His written word, the Bible *(2 Timothy 3:16-17; 2 Peter 1:16-21)*, and through His Son *(John 14:9)* that we can enter into a meaningful relationship with Him. But this is only possible when the barrier of one's sin has been removed by coming to trust in Christ's person and work on the cross as payment for one's sin. This is necessary because, as it is impossible for both light and darkness to dwell together, so it is impossible for a holy God to have fellowship with sinful mankind unless our sin has been paid for and removed. Jesus Christ, the sinless Son of God, died on the cross to take our punishment and change us so that the one who believes on Him can become a child of God and live eternally in His presence *(John 1:12; 2 Corinthians 5:21; 2 Peter 3:18; Romans 3:10-26)*.

There have been times in the past that God has revealed Himself more "visibly" to people. One example of this is at the time of the exodus from Egypt, when God revealed His care for the Israelites by sending the miraculous plagues upon the Egyptians until they were willing to release the Israelites from their slavery. God then opened up the Red Sea, enabling the approximately two million Israelites to cross over on dry ground. Then, as the Egyptian army sought to pursue them through the same opening, He defeated this enemy by bringing the waters upon them. Later, in the wilderness, God fed them miraculously with manna, guided them in the day by a pillar of cloud and by night by a pillar of fire, visible representations of His presence with them. He also obtained water for this great number of people in the wilderness through miraculous means, including causing water to flow from a rock as Moses struck it with his rod.

Yet, in spite of these repeated demonstrations of His love, guidance, and power, they still refused to trust Him when He wanted them to enter into the Promised Land. They chose instead to trust the word of ten men who frightened them with their stories of the walled cities and the giant stature of some of the people of the land, and to ignore the counsel of two godly men who encouraged them to trust God who had always been faithful. These events, found in the books of *Exodus* and *Numbers*, show that God's further revealing Himself to us would have no greater effect on our ability to trust Him. For were God to interact in a similar fashion with all of the people living today, we would respond no differently than did those Israelites...our sinful hearts are the same as theirs. But even as a few of the Israelites chose to trust God based on what He had revealed of Himself in the past and were willing to trust Him for the future, (going into the Promised Land - *Numbers 13:1 -14:9*), so we can choose to trust Him for our future based upon what He has already revealed about Himself and His character.

The Bible also speaks of a future time when the glorified Christ will return to rule the earth from Jerusalem for 1,000 years *(Revelation 20:1 -10)*. More people will be born on the earth during that reign of Christ. He will rule with complete justice and righteousness, yet in spite of His perfect rule, the Bible states that at the end of the 1,000 years, Satan will have no trouble rising up an army of men to rebel against and to seek to overthrow Christ's rule. The future event of the millennium and the past event of the exodus reveal that the problem is not with God insufficiently revealing Himself to man; rather, the problem is with man's sinful heart rebelling against God's loving reign because it craves its own sinful self-rule.

God has revealed enough of His nature for us to be able to trust Him. He has declared and shown through the events of history, in the workings of nature, and through the life of His only-begotten Son, Jesus Christ, that He is all-powerful, all-knowing, all-wise, all-loving, all-holy, unchanging, and eternal. And in that revelation, He has shown that He is worthy to be trusted. But as with the Israelites in the wilderness, the choice is ours as to whether or not we will trust Him. Often, one is inclined to make this choice based on what he/she thinks he knows about God rather than what He has revealed about Himself and can be understood about Him through a careful study of His inerrant word, the Bible. I encourage you to begin this careful study of the Bible, that you may come to know God through reliance upon His Son, Jesus Christ, who came to earth to save us from our sin so that we might have sweet companionship with God both now and in a fuller way in heaven one day.

53. Question: "God helps those who help themselves - is it in the Bible?"

"God helps those who help themselves" is probably the most often quoted phrase that is not found in the Bible. This is actually a quote from Ben Franklin and it appeared in Poor Richard's Almanac in 1757. In fact the Bible teaches the opposite. God helps the helpless! *Isaiah 25:4* declares, *"For You have been a defense for the helpless, a defense for the needy in his distress, a refuge from the storm, a shade from the heat..." Romans 5:6* tells us, *"For while we were still helpless, at the right time Christ died for the ungodly."*

In terms of salvation, we are all utterly helpless. We are all infected by sin *(Romans 3:23)*, and condemned as a result of that sin *(Romans 6:23)*. Nothing we can do on our own can remedy this situation *(Isaiah 64:6)*. Thankfully, God is the helper of the helpless. While we were still sinners, Jesus died for us *(Romans 5:8)*. Jesus paid the penalty that we were incapable of paying *(2 Corinthians 5:21)*. God provided the "help" that we need precisely because we could not help ourselves.

Apart from salvation, there is perhaps a way that the concept "God helps those who help themselves" is correct. As an example, if you asked me to help you move a piece of furniture, but then just watched me as I moved the furniture for you, I was not actually helping you. I would be doing the work for you. Many Christians fall into the trap of inactivity. Many Christians ask God for help, but then expect God to do everything Himself. They excuse this by pointing to the fact that God will provide according to His will and in His timing. However, this is not a reason for inactivity. As a specific example, if you are in need of a job, ask the Lord to help you find a job - but then be active in actually looking for a job. While it is in His power to do so, it is highly unlikely that God will cause employers to come looking for you!

54. Question: "Why does God allow birth defects?"

The ultimate answer to this difficult question is that when Adam and Eve sinned (Genesis chapter 3), they brought evil, sickness, disease, and death into the world. Sin has been wreaking havoc on the human race ever since. Birth defects occur because of sin...not because of sins the parents or the baby have committed, but because of sin itself. The hard part of the question is why God allows people to be born with terrible birth defects and/or deformities. Why doesn't God prevent birth defects from occurring?

The book of Job deals with the issue of not understanding why God allows certain things to occur. God had allowed Satan to do everything he wanted to Job except kill him. What was Job's reaction? "Though he slay me, yet will I hope in him" (Job 13:15). "The LORD gave and the LORD has taken away; may the name of the LORD be praised" (Job 1:21). Job didn't understand why God had allowed the things He did, but he knew that God was good and therefore continued to trust in Him. Ultimately, that should be our reaction as well. God is good, just, loving, and merciful. Often things happen to us that we simply cannot understand. However, instead of doubting God's goodness, our reaction should be to trust Him. "Trust in the LORD with all your heart and lean not on your own understanding; in all your ways acknowledge Him, and He will make your paths straight" (Proverbs 3:5-6).

Ultimately, the answer to this question has to be "I don't know." We will never be able to fully understand God and His ways. It is wrong for us to question why God allows something to occur. We simply have to trust that He is loving, good, and merciful - just like Job did - even when the evidence seems to indicate the opposite. Sickness and disease are the result of sin. God provided the "cure" for sin in sending Jesus Christ to die for us *(Romans 5:8)*. Once we are in heaven, we will be free from sickness, disease, and death. Until that day, we will have to deal with sin, its effects, and its consequences. We can praise God, though, that He can and will use birth defects and other tragedies for our good and His glory. *John 9:2 & 3* declares, *"His disciples asked Him, 'Rabbi, who sinned, this man or his parents, that he was born blind?' 'Neither this man nor his parents sinned,' said Jesus, 'but this happened so that the work of God might be displayed in his life.'*

55. Question: "Why does Scripture emphasize the right hand of God?"

The Scripture has several words translated "right" and the usage of the term, "right hand" ranges from a direction, to the opposite of wrong, what is just or what conforms to an established standard, and to a place of honor or authority. In the case of division or appointment in the Bible, the right hand or right side came first, as when Israel (Jacob) divided the blessings to Joseph's sons before he died (*Genesis 48:13 & 14*).

In addition, a person of high rank who put someone on his right hand gave him equal honor with himself and recognized him as possessing equal dignity and authority. And this is what the Apostle Paul writes of Jesus Christ *"And what is the surpassing greatness of His power toward us, the ones believing according to the working of His mighty strength which He worked in Christ in raising Him from the dead, and He seated Him at His right hand in the heavenlies, far above all principality and authority and power and dominion, and every name being named, not only in this world, but also in the coming age" (Ephesians 1:19-21).* Here we see God exalting Jesus above all others by seating Him at the right hand of the Father.

The term "God's right hand" in prophecy refers to the Messiah to whom is given the power and authority to subdue His enemies (*Psalm 110:1; Psalm 118:16*). We find a quote in *Matthew 22:44* from *Psalm 110:1*, which is a Messianic Psalm. *"The Son of David"* is claimed by the LORD Jesus Christ as He is the *"greater son of David"* or the Messiah. In this passage of *Matthew 22,* Jesus questions the Pharisees about who they think the "Christ" or the Messiah is. *"While the Pharisees were gathered together, Jesus asked them, Saying, What think ye of Christ? Whose son is He? They say unto him, The Son of David. He saith unto them, how then doth David in spirit call him Lord, saying, The LORD said unto my Lord, Sit thou on my right hand, till I make Thine enemies thy footstool? If David then call Him Lord, how is He his son?" (Matthew 22:41-45).* The position of the Messiah is at God's right hand.

The fact that Jesus Christ is at the "right hand of God" was a sign to the disciples that Jesus had indeed gone to heaven. In *John 16:7-15*, Jesus told the disciples that He had to go away and He would send the Holy Spirit. So the coming of the Holy Spirit in the upper room on the day of Pentecost (*Acts 2:1-13*) was proof positive that Jesus was indeed in heaven seated at the right hand of God. This is confirmed in *Romans 8:34* where the Apostle Paul writes that Christ is sitting at God's right hand making intercession for us.

Therefore, what we can say is that "God's right hand" refers to the Messiah, the LORD Jesus Christ and He is of equal position, honor, power and authority with God (*John 1:1-5*). The fact that Christ is "sitting" refers to the fact that His work of redemption is done and when the fullness of the gentiles is brought in (*Romans 11:25*), Christ's enemies will be made His footstool as the end of the age comes, all prophecy is completed, and time is no more.

56. Question: "Does God have a physical body?"

Both the Bible and good philosophy report that God is non-physical - spirit. In *John 4:24* it is said that God is spirit (see also *Luke 24:39; Romans 1:20; Colossians 1:15; 1 Timothy 1:17*). This is why no material thing was to be used to represent God (*Exodus 20:4*). But this can also be shown by reflecting on what God is. Philosophically the same truth comes through. All that is created is necessarily finite and limited. But the first cause (God) is uncreated, and therefore must be non-finite, or infinite. That which is beyond the finite must, by definition, be infinite, and the Bible states that God is beyond creation (*1 Kings 8:27; Job 11:7-9; Isaiah 66:1-2; Colossians 1:17*). That which is physical cannot be infinite - for you cannot add finite parts together until they reach infinity. Therefore God is spirit as opposed to physical/material in His Being. This does not mean He cannot localize a physical appearance. God is not composed of matter nor any other imaginable substance. He also cannot be measured, is not spatial, and has no true location (presence is a different concept).

Knowing this truth can help us understand the metaphorical speech often used to describe God or, more often, God's actions in Scripture. In the case of God, once all finitude is negated from a statement, what is left is what is actually true. If nothing is left, then it is a pure metaphor. Some metaphors use attributes from creation itself (*2 Samuel*

22:3). Others use man's attributes (anthropomorphism - *Deuteronomy 33:27*). In this way we can go from what we know by experience to what we know through the metaphors. For example, when Scripture describes God's mighty arm we know that arms are by definition limited - but might is not. So God's mighty arm is actually unlimited power to act (what we call omnipotence). When Scripture describes God's mind, we know that minds are limited, but knowledge is not. God's mind is actually His infinite knowledge (what we call omniscience).

There were times in the Bible when God appeared in a physical body in order to be seen by men in a form which they could perceive without danger to themselves. Because God said, *"No man can see me and live" (Exodus 33:20)*, He chose at certain times to reveal Himself in human form. These occurrences are called theophanies (*Genesis 12:7-9; 18:1-33; 32:22-30*). Every theophany wherein God takes on human form foreshadows the incarnation, where God took the form of a man to live among us as Emmanuel, "God with us" *(Matthew 1:23)*.

57. Question: "Can God sin? If God cannot sin, is He truly omnipotent?"

To answer this question, we must first consider who God is. The human mind, however, cannot adequately grasp who He is if it were not for the special revelations He has given us. One avenue of revelation is through God's creation *(Psalm 19:1-6)*. Creation's complexity, design, and order lead us to acknowledge there is an awesome Being who brought it into existence and maintains it.

Another avenue is through God's written Word. From scripture portions, we may ascertain the attributes, or qualities, that are inherent in God, thus giving us a glimpse of His character. One theologian states that His attributes are "His perfections." Some of them are: His eternality *(Psalm 90:2)*; His immutability, or unchanging quality *(James 1:17)*; His love *(1 John 4:8)*; His omnipotence, or being all powerful, the Almighty One *(Revelation 1:8)*; His omnipresence, or being everywhere present at all times *(Psalm 139:7-11)*; His holiness, absolute purity and separation from evil (*Habakkuk 1:13*); His righteousness, or justice (*Psalm 11:7*); and His truth (*Titus 1:2*).

This is a brief picture of God who manifested Himself in three persons, Father, Son and Holy Spirit, and the attributes, or perfections, are true for each member of the Godhead. Because God is holy, righteous and true, and He can do nothing inconsistent with Himself, we come to the conclusion that God cannot sin. Since holiness, righteousness, and God's other perfections are who God is, if God were to sin, He would cease to be God. The fact that God is "holy, holy, holy" prevents Him from doing anything that is unholy, i.e. sinful.

We cannot close, however, without realizing the amazing fact that our holy God involved Himself in mankind's sin. He sent His one and only Son to this earth to die to pay sin's penalty. *"For Christ died for sins once for all, the righteous for the unrighteous, to bring you to God" (1 Peter 3:18). "He Himself bore our sins in His body on the tree, so that we might die to sins and live for righteousness; by His wounds you have been healed" (1 Peter 2:24). "All have sinned and fall short of the glory of God, and are justified freely by His grace through the re-demption that came by Christ Jesus. God presented Him as a sacrifice of atonement, through faith in His blood" (Romans 3:23-25).*

58. Question: "What does it mean that God is infinite?"

The infinite nature of God simply means that God exists outside of and is not limited by time or space. Infinite simply means "without limits." When we refer to God as "infinite," we generally refer to Him with terms like omniscience, omnipotence, omnipresence.

Omniscience means that God is all-knowing or that He has unlimited knowledge. His infinite knowledge is what qualifies Him as sovereign ruler and judge over all things. Not only does God know everything that will happen, but He also knows all things that could have possibly happened. Nothing takes God by surprise, and no one can hide his sin from Him. There are many verses in the Bible where God reveals this aspect of His nature. One such verse is *1 John 3:20: "...God is greater than our heart, and knows all things."*

Omnipotence means that God is all-powerful or that He has unlimited power. It is significant because it establishes God's ability to carry out His sovereign will. Because God is omnipotent and has infinite power, nothing can stop His decreed will from happening, and nothing can thwart or stop His divine purposes from being fulfilled. There are many verses in the Bible where God reveals this aspect of His nature. One such verse is *Psalm 115:3: "But our God is in the heavens; He does whatever He pleases."* Or when answering His disciples' question *"Then who can be saved?" (Matthew 19:25)* Jesus answers them, *"With men this is impossible, but with God all things are possible" (Matthew 19:26).*

Omnipresence means that God is always present. There is no place that you could go to escape God's presence. God is not limited by time or space. He is present at every point of time and space. It is significant because it establishes that God is eternal. God has always existed and will always exist. Before time began, God was. Before the world or even matter itself was created, God was. He has no beginning or end, and there was never a time He did not exist, nor will there be a time when He ceases to exist. Again, many verses in the Bible reveal this aspect of God's nature to us, and one of them is *Psalm 139:7-10: "Where can I go from Thy Spirit? Or where can I flee from Thy presence? If I ascend to heaven, Thou art there; If I make my bed in Sheol, behold, Thou art there. If I take the wings of the dawn, If I dwell in the remotest part of the sea, Even there Thy hand will lead me, And Thy right hand will lay hold of me."*

Because God is infinite, He is also said to be transcendent, which simply means that God is exceedingly far above creation, and is both greater than creation and independent of it. What this means is that God is so infinitely above and beyond us and our ability to fully comprehend that, had He not revealed Himself, we would not know or understand what He is like. But, thankfully, God has not left us in the dark about Himself. Instead, He has revealed Himself to us through both general revelation (creation and our conscience) and special revelation (the Written Word of God, the Bible, and the living Word of God, Jesus Christ). Therefore, we can know God, and we can know how to be reconciled to Him and how to live according to His will. Despite the fact that we are finite and God is infinite, we can know and understand God as He has revealed Himself to us.

59. Question: "Why does *Isaiah 45:7* say that God created evil?"

Isaiah 45:7 in the King James Version reads, *"I form the light, and create darkness: I make peace, and create evil: I the LORD do all these things."* How does *Isaiah 45:7* agree with the view that God did not create evil? There are two key facts that need to be considered:

A. **Translation -** The word translated "evil" is from a Hebrew word that means "adversity, affliction, calamity, distress, misery." Notice how the other major English Bible translations render the word: "disaster" (NIV, HCSB), "calamity" (NKJV, NAS, ESV), and "woe" (NRSV). The Hebrew word can refer to moral evil, and often does have this meaning in the Hebrew Scriptures. However, due to the diversity of possible definitions, it is unwise to assume that *"I create evil"* in *Isaiah 45:7* refers to God bringing moral evil into existence.

B. **Context -** The context of *Isaiah 45:7* makes it clear that something other than "bringing moral evil into existence" is in mind. The context of *Isaiah 45:7* is God rewarding Israel for obedience and punishing Israel for disobedience. God pours out salvation and blessings on those whom He favors. God brings judgment on those who continue to rebel against Him. *"Woe to him who quarrels with his Master" (Isaiah 45:9).* That is the person to whom God brings "evil" and "disaster." So, rather than saying that God created "moral evil," *Isaiah 45:7* is presenting a common theme of Scripture - that God brings disaster on those who continue in hard-hearted rebellion against Him.

60. Question: "Where is God now? Where is God when it hurts?"

The Bible teaches that God reigns over the nations from His holy throne in Heaven *(Psalm 47:8; Isaiah 6:1, 66:1; Hebrews 4:16)*. Even though we know that God's presence is in some sense uniquely in Heaven, the teachings of Scripture also make it clear that God is omnipresent (present everywhere at the same time). From the beginning of Scripture, we see the presence of God hovering over the earth, even when it was still formless and empty *(Genesis 1:2)*. God filled the world with His creation and His presence and glory continue to inhabit the whole earth *(Numbers 14:21)*. There are many examples throughout Scripture of God's presence moving amidst the earth, interacting with His creation *(Genesis 3:8, Deuteronomy 23:14, Exodus 3:2, 1 Kings 19:11-18, Luke 1:35, Acts 16:7)*. Hebrews 4:13 says, *"Nothing in all creation is hidden from God's sight. Everything is uncovered and laid bare before the eyes of him to whom we must given an account."* Jeremiah 23:24 exclaims, *" 'Can anyone hide in secret places so that I cannot see him?' declares the Lord. 'Do not I fill heaven and earth?' declares the Lord."* Psalm 139 is an amazing study in God's omnipresence.

A. **Where is God?** If you are a believer in Jesus Christ, God is with you, beside you, above you, and inside you. God's presence and watchful care never leaves you. If you are not a believer in Jesus Christ, God is right in front of you, inviting you, drawing you, offering you the love, mercy, and grace that He longs to give you. If you are unsure of your relationship with God through Jesus Christ, please read our article on how to "Get right with God." Perhaps a better question than "Where is God?" is "Where are you, in relationship to God?"

B. **Where is God when it hurts?** It seems we desire to know the answer to this question most when faced with painful trials and attacks of doubt. Even Jesus, during His crucifixion, asked, *"My God, my God, why have you forsaken me?" (Matthew 27:46)*. To the onlookers of that time, as well as to those who first read the story, it seems that God did forsake Jesus, so we obviously conclude that He will forsake us as well in our darkest moments. Yet, upon continued observation of the events that unfolded after the crucifixion, the truth was revealed that nothing can separate us from the love of God, not even death *(Romans 8:37-39)*. After Jesus was crucified, He was glorified *(1 Peter 1:21, Mark 16:6 & 19; Romans 4:24 & 25)*. From this example alone we can be assured that even when we do not feel God's presence in the midst of our pain, we can still believe His promise that He will never leave us nor forsake us *(Hebrews 13:5)*. "God sometimes permits what he hates to accomplish what he loves" (Joni Erickson Tada).

We put our trust in the fact that God does not lie, He never changes, and His word stands true forever *(Numbers 23:19, 1 Samuel 15:29, Psalm 110:4, Malachi 3:6, Hebrews 7:21, 13:8, James 1:17, 1 Peter 1:25)*. We do not lose heart over painful circumstances because we live by faith in every word that has proceeded from the mouth of God, not putting our hope in what is seen or perceived. We trust God that our light and momentary troubles are achieving for us an eternal glory that far outweighs all the suffering that we will endure on this earth. So, we fix our eyes not on what is seen, but on what is unseen, because we know and believe that what is seen is temporary, but what is unseen is eternal *(2 Corinthians 4:16-18, 5:7)*. We also trust God's Word which says He is constantly working things together for the good of those who love Him and have been called according to his purpose *(Romans 8:28)*. Even though we do not always see the good ends to which God is working things out, we can be assured that a time will come when we will understand and see more clearly.

Our lives are like the illustration of a quilt. If you look at the back side of a quilt, all you see is a mess of knots and loose ends hanging out all over. It is very unattractive and there seems to be no rhyme or reason to the work. Yet when you turn the quilt over, you see how the maker has craftily woven together each strand to form a beautiful creation, much like the life of a believer *(Isaiah 64:8)*. We live with a limited understanding for the things of God, yet a day is coming when we will know and understand all things *(Job 37:5, Isaiah 40:28 Ecclesiastes 11:5, 1 Corinthians 13:12, 1 John 3:2)*. Where is God when it hurts? The message to take with you in hard times is that when you can't see His hand, trust His heart, and know for certain that He has not forsaken you. When you seem to have no strength of your own, that's when you can most fully rest in His presence and know that His strength is made perfect in your weakness (*2 Corinthians 12:9-10*).

61. Question: "Does God want us to worship Him as Father?"

The true God deserves and desires our worship with our inner selves and as He truly is. *"God is spirit, and those who worship Him must worship Him in spirit and in truth" (John 4:24).*

The truths of God, preserved for mankind in the Christian Bible, point to the door through which we can approach and worship the holy God from whom our sin has alienated us. Jesus said, *"No one comes to the Father but through me" (John 14:6b)* and also *"I am the door, by me if anyone enters in, he will be saved" (John 10:9).*

Our response, with our true inner selves and with sorrow for having sinned against God, is to approach Him in Jesus' name. God will forgive our sins because of Jesus Christ's sacrificial death on the cross. Through a new inner birth by His Spirit, He will make us a member of His family. Then, having become His own spiritual children, we can pray, *"Our Father in heaven" (Matthew 6:9a)*, worship that pleases Him.

62. Question: "Is it sometimes God's will for believers to be sick?"

The biblical doctrine of the sovereignty of God states that God is almighty over all. He is in complete control of all things; past, present and future; and nothing happens that is out of His jurisdiction. Either He directly causes, or He passively allows, everything that happens. But allowing something to happen and causing something to happen are two different things. For example, God caused the creation of the perfect, sinless Adam and Eve, and then He allowed them to rebel against Him. He did not cause them to sin and He certainly could have stopped them, but He chose not to for His own purposes and to bring about His perfect plan. That rebellion brought about all manner of evil, evil that was not caused by God, but which was allowed by Him to exist.

Sickness is one manifestation of the two broad types of evil, moral and natural. Moral evil is man's inhumanity to man. Natural evil is composed of things like natural disasters and physical sickness. Evil itself is a perversion or corruption of something that was originally good, but is now missing something. In the case of sickness, illness is a state where good health is missing. The Greek word for evil (ponerous) actually implies a malignancy, something that is corrupting a good and healthy state of being.

When Adam sinned, he condemned all of humanity to suffer the consequences of that sin, one of which is sickness. *Romans 8:20-22* says, *"For the creation was subjected to frustration, not by its own choice, but by the will of the one who subjected it, in hope that the creation itself will be liberated from its bondage to decay and brought into the glorious freedom of the children of God. We know that the whole creation has been groaning as in the pains of childbirth right up to the present time."* God, the *"one who subjected"* the creation to frustration following the Fall, did so in order to eventually liberate it from its bondage of sin, just as He liberates us from that bondage through Christ.

In the meantime, God uses sickness and other evils to bring about His sovereign purpose, to glorify Himself, and to exalt His holy name. At times, He miraculously heals sickness. Jesus went through Israel healing all manner of sickness and disease *(Matthew 4:23)* and even raised Lazarus from the dead after illness killed him, and Peter raised Dorcas from the dead *(Acts 9)*. At other times, He uses it as a method of discipline or as a judgment against sin. King Uzziah in the Old Testament was struck with leprosy *(2 Chronicles 26:19 & 20)*. Nebuchadnezzar was driven to madness by God until he came to understand that "the Most High rules in the affairs of men" *(Daniel 4)*. Herod was struck down and eaten by worms because he took God's glory upon himself *(Acts 12:21-23)*. There is even at least one case where God allowed disease, blindness, not as punishment for sin, but to reveal Himself and His mighty works through that blindness *(John 9:1-3)*.

When illness does come, it may not be the result of God's direct intervention in our lives, but is rather the result of the fallen world, fallen bodies, and poor health and lifestyle choices. And although there are scriptural indicators that God wants us to be in good health, *(3 John 2)* *"Beloved, I pray that in all respects you may prosper and be in good health, just as your soul prospers,"* all sickness and disease are allowed by Him for His purposes, whether we understand them or not.

Sickness is certainly the result of the Fall of man into sin, but God is very much in control and He does indeed determine how far evil can go. Just as He did with Satan and Job's trials; Satan was not allowed to exceed those boundaries. He tells us He is all-powerful some fifty-six times in the Bible, and it is amazing to see how His sovereignty dovetails with the choices we make, both bad and good, to work out in a perfect plan *(Romans 8:28)*.

For those who are believers and suffering with illnesses such as cancer in this life, the knowledge that they can glorify God through their suffering tempers the uncertainty as to why He has allowed it, something they may not truly understand until they stand in His presence in eternity. At that time, all questions will be answered.

63. Question: "What is the key to truly knowing God?"

Within all of us there exists a strong desire to be known and to know others. More importantly, all people desire to know their Creator, even if they are not professed believers in God. Today we are bombarded with advertising that promises many ways to satisfy our cravings to know more, to have more, to be more. However, the empty promises that come from the world will never satisfy in the way that knowing God will satisfy. Jesus said, *"Now this is eternal life: that they may know you, the only true God, and Jesus Christ, whom you have sent" (John 17:3).*

So "What is the key to truly knowing God?" First, it is imperative to understand that man, on his own, is incapable of truly knowing God because of his sinfulness. The Scriptures reveal to us that we are all sinful (*Romans 3*) and that we fall well short of the standard of holiness required to commune with God. We are also told that the consequence of our sin is death (*Romans 6:23*) and that we will perish eternally without God unless we accept and receive the promise of Jesus' sacrifice on the cross. So, in order to truly know God, we must first receive Him into our lives. *"As many as received Him, to them He gave the right to become children of God, even to those who believe in His name" (John 1:12).* Nothing is of greater importance than understanding this truth when it comes to knowing God. Jesus makes it clear that He alone is the way to heaven and knowing God personally when He states, *"I am the way, and the truth, and the life; no one comes to the Father, but through Me" (John 14:6).*

There is no requirement to begin this journey outside of repenting of sin and accepting and receiving the promises mentioned above. Jesus came to breathe life into us by offering Himself as a sacrifice so our sins will not prevent us from knowing God. Once we have received this truth, we can then begin the journey of knowing God in a personal way. One of the key ingredients in this journey is understanding that the Bible is God's Word and is His revelation of Himself, His promises, His will. The Bible is essentially a love letter written to us from a loving God who created us to know Him intimately. What better way to learn about our Creator than to immerse ourselves in His Word, revealed to us for this very reason? And it is important to continue this process throughout the entire journey. Paul writes to Timothy, *"But as for you, continue in what you have learned and have become convinced of, because you know those from whom you learned it, and how from infancy you have known the Holy Scriptures, which are able to make you wise for salvation through faith in Christ Jesus. All Scripture is God-breathed and is useful for teaching, rebuking, correcting and training in righteousness, so that the man of God may be thoroughly equipped for every good work" (1 Timothy 3:16).*

Finally, truly knowing God involves our commitment to obedience to what we read in the Scriptures. After all, we were created to do good works (*Ephesians 2:10*), in order to be part of God's plan of continuing to reveal Himself to the world. We carry the responsibility to live out the very faith that is required to know God. We are salt and light on this earth (*Matthew 5:13 & 14*), designed to bring God's flavor to the world and to serve as a shining light in the midst of darkness. Not only must we read and understand God's Word, we must apply it obediently and remain faithful *(Hebrews 12)*. Jesus Himself placed the greatest importance on loving God with all we are and loving our neighbor as ourselves *(Matthew 22)*. This command is impossible to keep without the commitment to reading and applying His truth revealed to us in His Word.

These are the keys to truly knowing God. Of course, our lives will involve much more than just these few keys of truth, such as commitment to prayer, devotion, fellowship, and worship. But those can only follow making a decision to receive Jesus and His promises into our lives and accepting that we, on our own, cannot truly know God. Then our lives can be filled with God and we can experience knowing Him intimately and personally.

64. Question: "How is belief in God any different from Flying Spaghetti Monsterism?"

Flying Spaghetti Monsterism (also known as Pastafarianism) is a "religion" created by a man named Bobby Henderson. Mr. Henderson created this satire in protest of the Kansas State Board of Education's decision to teach intelligent design as an alternative to the theory of evolution. In essence, he was asking, "If foolish religious ideas like that of Intelligent Design have to be given equal time in high school biology classes, then why can't other foolish religious ideas be taught alongside with it?" So, in protest, he made up a silly set of religious beliefs and demanded that they be given equal time in biology classes alongside the theories of evolution and Intelligent Design. His point seems to be that to teach Intelligent Design in schools is as absurd as teaching that the Flying Spaghetti Monster made the world and deceived scientists into believing evolution. (Note: Flying Spaghetti Monsterism is simply a new, and more entertaining, variation of Russell's teapot and the Invisible Pink Unicorn.)

The line of reasoning for Flying Spaghetti Monsterism seems to be that

    A. There is no evidence for the existence of the Judeo-Christian God.

    B. There is no evidence for the existence of the Flying

Spaghetti Monster.

C. Therefore, belief in the Judeo-Christian God and belief in the Flying Spaghetti Monster are on equal epistemic grounds.

There are more problems with this thinking than can be covered in this article. However, some responses should given.

Premise A is false. It is not the case that "there is no evidence for the existence of the Judeo-Christian God." Mr. Henderson may not accept the evidence for the existence of the Judeo-Christian God, but he does not offer much by way of demonstrating that the classical and contemporary arguments for God's existence are false. Even if he adequately refuted several arguments given by theists for the belief in God, he would still not be justified in saying that "there is NO evidence for the existence of God." In fact, this comment smacks of a priori rejection (a rejection of the evidence before the evidence is even given) of the notion that evidence may be given for the existence of God.

Many arguments have been given for the existence of God. For example, there are cosmological arguments (arguments for a first cause), teleological arguments (arguments for a Grand Designer), moral arguments (arguments for a Moral Lawgiver), and others. Anyone who is serious about the question of God must deal with these arguments charitably and thoroughly before dogmatically rejecting belief in God. To ignorantly reject the existence of God "because I can't think of any good reasons to believe in God" is not in keeping with the most influential thinkers in Western civilization. Almost all major philosophers and thinkers have dealt with the existence of God, and most of them accepted some form of belief in a God. A large number of philosophers have argued for their belief in the existence of God. It is a small minority of thinkers who have denied the existence of God.

NOTE: This is not advocating the "appeal to the people" fallacy (argumentum ad populum). The argument is not that belief in God is true BECAUSE so many people believe that God exists. Rather, it is simply an irrefutable fact that many brilliant minds have pondered the God question and come to the conclusion that He does, in fact, exist. This fact, while it doesn't prove that God exists, should prompt us to deal with the question of God's existence with seriousness and intellectual honesty.

In contrast with the serious issue of God's existence, Flying Spaghetti Monsterism is known to be made up. Several contrasts between belief in God and belief in the Flying Spaghetti Monster are listed below:

Belief in God
- ⇒ Prevalent among all peoples of all times. Atheism is very rare; even atheists admit this.
- ⇒ There are many sophisticated philosophical arguments for God's existence.
- ⇒ The Christian God is a coherent explanation of why something exists rather than nothing, why logic is prescriptive and universal, why morality is objective, and why religion is ubiquitous.
- ⇒ Belief in God is rationally satisfying.

Belief in Flying Spaghetti Monsterism
- ⇒ Believed by no one. Even the so-called advocates of the FSM do not really believe that it exists.
- ⇒ There are no technical philosophical arguments for the FSM. Actually, there are no technical arguments of any kind for the FSM.
- ⇒ Even those who sarcastically espouse that the FSM exists don't really believe that the FSM exists, nor do they think that the FSM is a coherent explanation for finite contingent being, logic, morality, beauty, etc.
- ⇒ No one really believes in the FSM, but even if they did, it would not be rationally satisfying.

While there are some atheists who take theistic arguments seriously, many atheists do not take the time to seriously consider these arguments. This fact may be clearly seen in popular atheist texts (e.g., The Atheist Debater's Handbook and The God Delusion). These texts refute weak and incomplete arguments for theism and suppose that they have refuted the actual, fully reasoned arguments that Christian philosophers and theologians give. This is an intellectually dishonest practice.

In short, the difference between belief in God and belief in the Flying Spaghetti Monster is this:

Belief in God is rational and supported by good reasons, and belief in the Flying Spaghetti Monster is irrational and not supported by any good reasons. Bobby Henderson simply begs the question (commits a logical fallacy) when he says that there are no good reasons for belief in God. Despite his claim to the contrary, Christianity is a rationally defensible religion. There are difficult questions that we must ask ourselves as Christians, but the fact that there are difficult questions is not grounds for dismissing Christianity. As believers, our pursuit of answers to our own deep-seated spiritual questions draws us further into the intellectual richness of the Christian faith.

64. Question: "Why won't God heal amputees?"

Some use this question in an attempt to "disprove" the existence of God. In fact, there is a popular anti-Christian website dedicated to the "Why won't God heal amputees?" argument: If God is all-powerful and if Jesus promised to do anything we ask (or so the reasoning goes), then why won't God ever heal amputees when we pray for them? Why does God heal victims of cancer and diabetes, for example, yet He never causes an amputated limb to be regenerated? The fact that an amputee stays an amputee is "proof" to some that God does not exist, that prayer is useless, that so-called healings are coincidence, and that religion is a myth.

The above argument is usually presented in a thoughtful, well-reasoned way, with a liberal sprinkling of Scripture to make it seem all the more legitimate. However, it is an argument based on a wrong view of God and a misrepresentation of Scripture. The line of reasoning employed in the "why won't God heal amputees" argument makes at least seven false assumptions:

A. **God has never healed an amputee.** Who is to say that in the history of the world, God has never caused a limb to regenerate? To say, "I have no empirical evidence that limbs can regenerate; therefore, no amputee has ever been healed in the history of the world" is akin to saying "I have no empirical evidence that rabbits live in my yard; therefore, no rabbit has ever lived on this ground in the history of the world." It's a conclusion that simply cannot be drawn. Besides, we have the historical record of Jesus healing lepers, some of whom we may assume had lost digits or facial features. In each case, the lepers were restored whole (*Mark 1:40-42; Luke 17:12-14*). Also, there is the case of the man with the shriveled hand (*Matthew 12:9-13*), and the restoration of Malchus's severed ear (*Luke 22:50-51*), not to mention the fact that Jesus raised the dead (*Matthew 11:5; John 11*), which would undeniably be even more difficult than healing an amputee.

B. God's goodness and love require Him to heal everyone. Illness, suffering, and pain are the result of our living in a cursed world, cursed because of our sin (*Genesis 3:16-19; Romans 8:20-22*). God's goodness and love moved Him to provide a Savior to redeem us from the curse (*1 John 4:9 & 10*), but our ultimate redemption will not be realized until God has made a final end of sin in the world. Until that time, we are still subject to physical death.

If God's love required Him to heal every disease and infirmity, then no one would ever die, because "love" would maintain everyone in perfect health. The biblical definition of love is "a sacrificial seeking of what is best for the loved one." What is best for us is not always physical wholeness. Paul the apostle prayed to have his "thorn in the flesh" removed, but God said, "No" because He wanted Paul to understand he didn't need to be physically whole to experience the sustaining grace of God. Through the experience, Paul grew in humility and in the understanding of God's mercy and power (*2 Corinthians 12:7-10*).

The testimony of Joni Eareckson Tada provides a modern example of what God can do through physical tragedy. As a teenager, Joni suffered a diving accident that left her a quadriplegic. In her book Joni, she relates how she visited faith healers many times and prayed desperately for the healing which never came. Finally, she accepted her condition as God's will, and she writes, "The more I think about it, the more I'm convinced that God doesn't want everyone well. He uses our problems for His glory and our good" (p. 190).

C. God still performs miracles today just as He did in the past. In the thousands of years of history covered by the Bible, we find just four short periods in which miracles were widely performed (the period of the Exodus, the time of the prophets Elijah and Elisha, the ministry of Jesus, and the time of the apostles). While miracles occurred throughout the Bible, it was only during these four periods that miracles were "common."

The time of the apostles ended with the writing of Revelation and the death of John. That means that now miracles are once again rare. Any ministry which claims to be led by a new breed of apostle or claims to possess the ability to heal is deceiving people. "Faith healers" play upon emotion and use the power of suggestion to produce unverifiable "healings." This is not to say that God does not heal people today, we believe He does, but not in the numbers or in the way that some people claim.

We turn again to the story of Joni Eareckson Tada, who at one time sought the help of faith healers. On the subject of modern-day miracles, she says, "Man's dealing with God in our day and culture is based on His Word rather than 'signs and wonders'" (op cit., p. 190). His grace is sufficient, and His Word is sure.

D. God is bound to say "yes" to any prayer offered in faith. Jesus said, *"I am going to the Father. And I will do whatever you ask in my name, so that the Son may bring glory to the Father. You may ask me for anything in my name, and I will do it" (John 14:12-14).* Some have tried to interpret this passage as a carte blanche from Jesus promising His agreement to whatever we ask. But this is misreading Jesus' intent. Notice, first, that Jesus is speaking to His apostles, and the promise is for them. After Jesus' ascension, the apostles were given power to perform miracles as they spread the gospel (*Acts 5:12*). Second, Jesus twice uses the phrase "in My name." This indicates the basis for the apostles' prayers, but it also implies that whatever they prayed for should be consonant with Jesus' will. A selfish prayer, for example, or one motivated by greed, cannot be said to be prayed in Jesus' name.

We pray in faith, but faith means that we trust God. We trust Him to do what is best and to know what is best. When we consider all the Bible's teaching on prayer, not just the promise given to the apostles, we learn that God may exercise His power in response to our prayer, or He may surprise us with a different course of action. In His wisdom He always does what is best (*Romans 8:28*).

E. **God's future healing, at the resurrection, cannot compensate for earthly suffering.** The truth is, *"our present sufferings are not worth comparing with the glory that will be revealed in us" (Romans 8:18)*. When a believer loses a limb, he has God's promise of future wholeness, and faith is *"being sure of what we hope for and certain of what we do not see" (Hebrews 11:4)*. Jesus said, *"It is better for you to enter life maimed or crippled than to have two hands or two feet and be thrown into eternal fire" (Matthew 18:8)*. His words confirm the relative unimportance of our physical condition in this world, as compared to our eternal state. To enter life maimed, and then to be made whole, is infinitely better than to enter hell whole and suffer for eternity.

F. **God's plan is subject to man's approval.** One of the contentions of the "why won't God heal amputees" argument is that God just isn't "fair" to amputees. Yet, Scripture is clear that God is perfectly just (*Psalm 11:7; 2 Thessalonians 1:5 & 6*) and in His sovereignty answers to no one (*Romans 9:20 & 21*). A believer has faith in God's goodness, even when circumstances make it difficult and reason seems to falter.

G. **God does not exist.** This is the underlying assumption on which the whole "why won't God heal amputees" argument is based. Those who champion the "why won't God heal amputees" argument start with the assumption that God does not exist and then proceed to buttress their idea as best they can. For them, "religion is a myth" is a foregone conclusion, presented as a logical deduction but which is, in reality, foundational to the argument.

In one sense, the question of why God doesn't heal amputees is a "gotcha" question, comparable to "Can God make a rock too big for Him to lift?" and is designed not to seek for truth but to discredit faith. In another sense, it can be a valid question with a biblical answer. That answer, in short, would be something like this: "God can heal amputees and will heal every one of them who trusts Christ as Savior. The healing will come, not as the result of our demanding it now, but in God's own time, possibly in this life, but definitely in Heaven. Until that time, we walk by faith, trusting the God who redeems us in Christ and promises the resurrection of the body."

65. Question: "Is God cruel?"

There are atheists and agnostics who argue that the God who is presented in the Bible is cruel. For example, the online Skeptics Annotated Bible has an entire section devoted to biblical passages that, they claim, demonstrate that God is cruel. By labeling God as cruel, they are appealing to our human, moral sensibilities. The word cruelty is defined as "callous indifference to, or pleasure in, causing pain and suffering." The question before us now is, Is God cruel? To answer in the affirmative, we would have to allow that God either doesn't care about pain and suffering, or He actually enjoys watching His creatures suffer.

The atheists / agnostics who claim that God is cruel have a large burden of proof. They are not merely claiming to know about the actions of God; they are also claiming to sufficiently know the circumstances in which He performed those actions, as well as His motivations. Additionally, they are claiming to know the very mind of God, ascribing to Him the attitudes of indifference and/or sadistic pleasure necessary to define Him as cruel. Quite frankly, this is beyond the skeptics' ability to demonstrate, they can't possibly know the mind of God. *"'For my thoughts are not your thoughts, neither are your ways my ways,' declares the LORD. 'As the heavens are higher than the earth, so are my ways higher than your ways and my thoughts than your thoughts'" (Isaiah 55:8-9).*

There is no doubt that God both allows and, at times, causes pain and suffering, but God's goodness cannot be impugned because He commits an act that appears cruel to us. While we can't claim to know His reasoning in every circumstance, we do know several reasons for actions that can appear to us to be cruel, especially if we don't know, or don't bother to find out, the circumstances:

A. **To mete out just punishment** - If a punishment is just, can it be said to be cruel? What critics usually do not understand is that God's love is not diminished when He brings punishment on people. God is able to bring judgment on an evil group of people in order to spare those who are devoted to Him. To allow evil and wrongdoing to go unpunished would indeed be cruel and would indicate a callousness toward the innocent. When God caused the Red Sea to close, drowning Pharaoh's entire army, He was punishing Pharaoh's rebellion against Him and preserving His chosen people from certain slaughter and annihilation (*Exodus 14*). Wrongdoing that does not result in punishment inevitably results in greater and greater wrongdoing, which benefits no one and is detrimental to the common good. Even when God told the Israelites to completely destroy the enemies of God, including women and children, He knew that to let them live would ensure the existence of future generations devoted to evil idolatrous practices including, in some cases, child sacrifices on the altars of false gods.

B. **To bring about a greater good**- Pain and suffering that produce a greater good sometimes can be brought about by no other means. The Bible tells us that trials and difficulties produce stronger, better Christians, and we should *"count it all joy" (James 1:2)* when we encounter them. God brings these about for our benefit, in order to refine us like gold in the fire of affliction. The Apostle Paul saw his own suffering, beatings, stonings, shipwrecks, hunger, thirst, cold, and imprisonments, as a means of ensuring that he would be ever conscious of his own weakness, would remember always that the power at work in him was from God, not himself, and would never be deluded into relying on his own power (*2 Corinthians 1:8-10; 4:7-12*). Against nonbelievers, God's justice is vindicated when He causes pain and suffering to them because they deserve it. He demonstrates His mercy to them by warning them repeatedly of the consequences of sin. When, through their own rebellion, they bring upon themselves calamity, this is just punishment, not cruelty. The fact that He lets rebels go on shaking their fists at Him as long as He does indicates His mercy and patience, not cruelty.

C. **To glorify Himself** - God is glorified by the exhibition of His attributes. We all agree that He looks pretty good to us when His love and mercy are on display, but since each and every attribute is holy and perfect, even the exhibition of His wrath and anger bring Him glory. And that is the ultimate goal, His glory not ours. Our tiny, finite brains can't even adequately imagine Him; much less call Him into question.

All these are worthy, valid, noble causes for pain and suffering. Contrary to the claims of skeptics, there are good reasons for God's allowing evil and suffering in this world. We are privileged to know some of those reasons, but we do not always know why God allows evil and suffering. To trust God in spite of not knowing the reasons is not a blind leap of faith. Rather, we trust Him with the things we don't understand because we see His faithfulness in those actions which we do understand.

If we read the Bible carefully, rather than seeing God act out of cruelty, we see Him acting out of His love for us. For example, the book of *Job* is often pointed to as an example of God's sadistic actions against an innocent man. The book declares that Job was innocent of the suffering that came upon him, which appears to favor the claim of the atheist. But to claim that it proves God is sadistic betrays a very superficial understanding of the book of *Job*.

In the Near East during the time of the patriarchs, a common belief was that God always blessed the righteous and brought suffering on the unrighteous. The book of *Job* is a polemic against that theology. The story shows that man's view of God's justice needed to be modified. We need to understand that God is not limited to using suffering as a means of retribution. He also uses it to tear people away from the earthly things that so easily entice them. Additionally, Job brings people closer to understanding God's work of atonement on the cross. If mankind continued to think that God couldn't allow an innocent man to suffer, then we would have missed God's plan for redeeming the world. For God allowed the suffering of a perfectly innocent Man (Jesus Christ) in order to bring His own to salvation. So this book of Job ends up being an invaluable contribution to the history of redemption.

In summary, the skeptic must bear a very large burden of proof in claiming that God's actions are characterized by cruelty. In context, the biblical passages which appear to paint God as cruel actually do no such thing. In fact, with a proper understanding of the Scriptures, we see that God's actions are always motivated by, and consistent with, His holy and perfect character.